Let's Face It

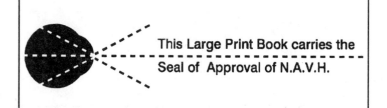

This Large Print Book carries the
Seal of Approval of N.A.V.H.

LET'S FACE IT

90 YEARS OF LIVING, LOVING, AND LEARNING

KIRK DOUGLAS

THORNDIKE PRESS

An imprint of Thomson Gale, a part of The Thomson Corporation

Detroit • New York • San Francisco • New Haven, Conn. • Waterville, Maine • London

THOMSON
™
GALE

LIBRARY OF CONGRESS CATALOGING-IN-PUBLICATION DATA

Douglas, Kirk, 1916–
   Let's face it : 90 years of living, loving, and learning / by Kirk Douglas.
      p. cm. — (Thorndike Press large print biography)
   ISBN-13: 978-0-7862-9814-3 (hardcover : lg. print : alk. paper)
   ISBN-10: 0-7862-9814-6 (hardcover : lg. print : alk. paper)
   1. Douglas, Kirk, 1916– 2. Motion picture actors and actresses — United States — Biography. 3. Large type books. I. Title.
PN2287.D54A3 2007b
792.02′8092—dc22   2007019788

Published in 2007 by arrangement with John Wiley & Sons, Inc.

Printed in the United States of America on permanent paper
10 9 8 7 6 5 4 3 2 1

This book is dedicated to my
grandchildren:
Cameron, Kelsey, Ryan, Tyler, Dylan,
Carys, and Jason.
Love,
Pappy

CONTENTS

FOREWORD

Kirk Douglas is the last surviving Hollywood global superstar, not counting a much-younger Clint Eastwood. These bigger-than-life characters reigned from the late 1930s to the early 1970s. Even now, their films on TV, cable, and DVD still appeal to people from all countries and cultures. I have known Kirk since 1963 (you do the arithmetic). After I became part of the film industry in 1966, Kirk and I bonded in a deep, loving, and loyal friendship that has resisted erosion.

Let's Face It (Kirk says it's his last book, but don't count on that) is sadness wrapped in humor inside a precious box of memories. Kirk's life has been a journey of fame only a tiny few are ever permitted to take. As Kirk has moved through nine decades of living, so many of those who were his collaborators and friends — famous names and faces with whom he shared exciting and

11

amusing times — are gone. The memories remain. He shares many of them in this book.

Kirk does it all with a melancholy dipped in a soft, subtle wit. Suddenly you finish a sentence and you're smiling if not laughing out loud. Despite Kirk's many collisions with disaster — a midair crash between his chopper and a small plane that caused him to fall a hundred feet to earth; a stroke that almost robbed him of his voice; a pacemaker that keeps pumping — his sense of humor is robustly intact. So is his passion. Kirk is still capable of outrage over the follies and stupidities of the human race.

I am so proud of my longtime friend. Kirk and his wife, Anne, and my wife, Mary Margaret, and I have traveled the world together. Wherever we go, in faraway places with strange-sounding names, he is recognized, embraced, and lauded. Even after all my years in the movie world, I am still astounded by Kirk's power to stir the affections of ordinary people. It is a miraculous power, and he wields it with grace.

— Jack Valenti

ACKNOWLEDGMENTS

Do real writers write books without help? I can't imagine it. I want to thank at least a few people who gave me help and encouragement:

David Wolpe, the rabbi of Sinai Temple, with whom I study religion an hour a week. Elli Wolpe, his wife, who helps me so much with her comments. Ushi Obst, my editor on my earlier books — a Catholic girl who converted to Judaism, went to Jerusalem, and married a rabbi. Don't blame me.

I can't pronounce my assistant Grace's last name, but I can spell it: Eboigbe. She was a big help. Not only did she untangle my mangled speech and put it in the computer, she was not shy about giving me her criticisms.

This is the first time I have worked with Walter Bode as my editor. Now I'm sorry that this is my last book because he has been such a great help. Thanks also to Alan Nevins, who encouraged me to write this book, and Tom Miller, who surprised me with his astute observations that have helped my book.

And, of course, my wife, Anne. I'm always walking a picket fence for her, hoping to make her smile in approval. She always laughs when I fall off.

INTRODUCTION

They say a rose by any other name would smell as sweet; then why do so many people change their names? Even Hitler changed his name from Schicklgruber. In the movies, some names are changed because they sound too Jewish, some because they sound too Italian, and others because they wouldn't look suitable on a marquee. This may be why Muzyad Yakhoob became Danny Thomas. How would you like to see the real name of Robert Taylor in lights: Spanger Arlington Brugh? And can you imagine calling John Wayne by his real name, Marion Morrison?

Of course everyone called him "Duke." When we were shooting *The War Wagon,* he said to me, "People call me Duke. You always call me John. Why?"

"John," I said, "I could never call you Duke. Maybe Prince or King, but Duke? Never."

Anyone can see why my friend Karl Malden from Gary, Indiana, changed his name from Mladen Sekulovich. The talented Fred Astaire also left behind his real name — Frederick Austerlitz. Archibald Alexander Leach assumed a new identity as Cary Grant. Another friend, Tony Curtis, used to be Bernard Schwartz.

If Antonio Dominic Benedetto sang "I Left My Heart in San Francisco," would it bring tears to my eyes as much as if Tony Bennett sang it?

Of course, for an actor, a name is a trademark, a brand. Actor's Equity even restricts the use of certain names. For instance, my son Michael Douglas ran into problems because his name had already been claimed by singer/actor Mike Douglas (whose real name was Mike Dowd). And you really have to feel for Michael Douglas (not my son), who had to change his name to Michael Keaton because of my son's success. Keaton also succeeded as an actor, so I guess it's all right.

Not so long ago, actors began to use their real ethnic names: Al Pacino, Robert De Niro, Jerry Seinfeld, David Schwimmer. More recently, there are Matthew McConaughey, Garry Shandling, Melina Kanakaredes, and many others. I applaud them. If

Arnold Schwarzenegger had come to Hollywood during my time, his name would have been changed to Arnold Black — *schwartz* means "black" in German. He didn't do badly with Schwarzenegger.

I never forgot my original name: Issur Danielovitch. When my father, Herschel (Harry) Danielovitch, left Russia to come to the small town of Amsterdam, New York, his brother in the United States was going under the name of Demsky. So my father became Harry Demsky, and I became Izzy Demsky. I always hated that name.

During one college vacation, I worked at a summer stock playhouse with Karl Malden (after he'd changed his name). He and the rest of the players debated what my name should be. I suggested Ivan Daniels, using the initials of my original name. They disagreed; they thought it should be a simple last name and an unusual first name. The director of our group blurted out, "Kirk Douglas." We all liked that name. Ivan Daniels was kicked out and Kirk Douglas stayed.

Before entering the navy, during World War II, I had my name legally changed to Kirk Douglas. Now, though, in the twilight of my years, I feel guilty for abandoning Issur Danielovitch. If I had become a ballet dancer, my name would have been perfect. So what the hell, I became an actor. Would Issur Danielovitch look so bad on the marquee?

I feel sorry for Issur. He never got a chance to have his say, and he never had his name on the cover of my books.

So, here's what Issur Danielovitch/Izzy Demsky/Kirk Douglas has to say after ninety years of becoming who he is.

1
MY BIRTHDAY

Have you ever seen a cake with ninety candles? It's huge! I thought it would take me a day and a half to blow out the candles, so I called on my sons to help me. As we huddled around the candles waiting for my count to three, I could see glints of silver in their hair reflected in the candlelight. That surprised me as we blew out the candles in one big puff.

My ninetieth birthday party took place at the L'Orangerie restaurant — that's where we had my eightieth birthday party and my eighty-ninth as well. I was flabbergasted by the party Anne had put together. Over a hundred friends attended. She had the barrier in the middle of the dining room removed and all the banquettes taken out. She had an upright piano put in and hired a three-piece orchestra to accompany the performers. The room was completely filled with tables decorated with beautiful flowers and candles. The meal was delicious.

I wasn't prepared for the show that my friend George Schlatter had arranged, either. Dennis Miller was the MC and he introduced my friend of forty-six years, Jack Valenti, who had some warm remarks to make. Don Rickles, whom I have known much longer, was hilarious as usual. Larry Gelbart, the comedy writer, did a very funny stand-up routine, and Larry's wife and Neile Toffel did a duet of one of my favorites, "Are You Lonesome Tonight?" They dragged me up to do one chorus with them. My daughter-in-law Catherine Zeta-Jones was ravishing as she sang "How Deep Is the Ocean, How High Is the Sky," another one of my favorite songs. She didn't ask me to come up and sing with her.

The hit of the show was introduced by a strolling violinist playing the music to *Fiddler on the Roof* as my three sons, Michael, Joel, and Peter, performed a song-and-dance routine parody. They were clumsy but very funny as they danced and sang:

Kirk cast a giant shadow
Through all seven days in May
Out of the past, this juggler
Played a great Doc Holliday
He crashed the walls of Jericho

'Cause they were in his way
All women dreamed to be with him
All men wished they were gay.

I thought a serious note was about to be injected into the festivities when my wife, Anne, got up with a glass in her hand to propose a toast. She spoke of "this wonderful man who is also my friend has just written a book" — I checked my fly and prepared to take a bow — *"Don Webster!"* Don is my ex-wife's husband and it was his birthday, too.

I sank back into my seat, but it was time for me to speak: "As you get older, memories become very important. I can remember a night, years ago, at a charity dinner. I was sitting next to my friend Burt Lancaster, and he said to me, 'Koik' — he always called me that — 'you're not eating.' I answered, 'Boit' — I always called him that — 'when I make a talk, I want my stomach to be empty and my brain full.' I then pointed to each part of my anatomy. After finishing my talk I returned to my table and Boit said, 'Koik, you could have eaten.' "

That got a big laugh, so I was encouraged to continue: "When I struggled with my tie tonight — I seldom wear ties — I nervously asked my wife, 'How do I look?' Her answer was 'You don't look a day over eighty-nine.' " Another laugh. I was getting very courageous. "When you get to ninety — I can't believe I have — you take inventory of your life. For the first time, you really appreciate friends. You know the meaning of what Shakespeare said: 'When you find a true friend, grapple him to your soul with hoops of steel.' All my friends here are locked to my soul with hoops of steel. You also think of the mistakes that you have made in life. Today I thought of one mistake that I can correct. A few years ago, on our fiftieth wedding anniversary, I married Anne again. I composed a poem and a song and lyrics to my wife for that precious day. Now I realize that my wife deserves more than some crappy verses that I wrote. She deserves the best — Shakespeare." Then I recited:

When, in disgrace with fortune and men's
    eyes,
I all alone beweep my outcast state
And trouble deaf heaven with my bootless
    cries
And look upon myself and curse my fate,
Wishing me like to one more rich in hope,
Featured like him, like him with friends
    possess'd,

Desiring that man's art and that man's
    scope,
With what I most enjoy contented least;
Yet in these thoughts myself almost de-
    spising,
Haply I think on thee, and then my state,
Like to the lark at break of day arising
From sullen earth, sings hymns at heav-
    en's gate;
For thy sweet love remember'd such
    wealth brings
That then I scorn to change my state with
    kings.

Many bottles of wine were consumed
before my friends reluctantly dispersed into
the beautiful rain-sprinkled night. The first
thing I did when we got home was go into
the garden to relieve myself in the bushes.
That's a secret pleasure all men keep from
women.

Anne was getting ready for bed. Through
the window she called to me, "What are you
doing out there, birthday boy?"

"I want to take a walk around the pool."

"Well, don't fall in. I would hate to ruin
my new gown." I chuckled, then she said
gently, "Get ready for bed, I'll take care of
the lights."

2
TWO HEADS ARE
BETTER THAN ONE

Ninety is old, you must agree, but I started feeling old two years ago when I was eighty-eight and they installed a dual bust in my garden. Eighty-eight, a strange number, contains the four circles of my life — childhood, youth, maturity, and old age. I have completed three of these circles, and I'm almost through the fourth. I'm writing my ninth book. It's difficult to accept that it will be my last book. It's even more difficult to accept that I am an old man. This book is my attempt to deal with that fact.

The dual bust in my garden was created by the artist Seward Johnson, who has known me ever since I first came out of the navy married to his aunt Diana. At the time I was about twenty-seven. He insisted on making a dual bust of me — a sculpture portraying me as I am now and the twenty-seven-year-old Kirk he remembers.

My grandchildren make jokes about it.

With my two-headed sculpture.

"Pappy," they say, "you look younger now than you did eighty years ago."

The poet Robert Browning once wrote, "Grow old along with me, the best is yet to be." Let's face it, that's a lot of crap! I have trouble walking, talking, seeing, and hearing. But I've made it this far.

Near the end of his life, John Adams said, "There is a ripeness of time for death regarding others as well as ourselves, when it is reasonable we should drop off and make room for another growth. When we have lived our generation out, we should not wish to encroach on another."

Oh, *really! I* don't feel that way.

It's very early. My wife's not awake yet. My dogs lie beside me as I sit in the garden by the pool sipping coffee. The pool is surrounded by five pieces of sculpture. I rarely look at them because they don't compare with the living sculpture of two giant avocado trees in a corner. One trunk is thick and dark, the other is slim and light, their giant branches entwined like lovers as they reach up to the sky. They are crowned by a mass of green leaves silver-tinted by the sun. The leaves act like a laurel wreath swaying in the breeze. Some of them fall to the ground, making way for new ones. I admire them, thinking of the poem that ends "Poems are made by fools like me, but only God can make a tree." I shift my eyes across the pool to my head — not one, but two heads.

The young Kirk was just out of the navy — egotistical, ambitious, with extraordinary physical abilities. He'd been an undefeated wrestler in college. In movies he insisted on doing his own stunts. After he had an accident, his back was X-rayed. The doctor

asked, "Kirk, do you do *all* your stunts?"
"Yes," young Kirk answered. "Why?"

"I can see all of them on your back."

Young Kirk also spent a lot of time — too much — in sexual pursuits. I don't like him very much. He was wrapped up in himself as he went from picture to picture. Of course, forming his own company in his thirties didn't help. Nobody likes the boss.

The older, mature Kirk became very different. After some near-death encounters — a midair collision between a light plane and a helicopter he was in, getting a pacemaker, having a stroke, and undergoing a potentially fatal double-knee operation — he began to think of other things besides himself. He began to think of God and became interested in helping other people. He discovered that the purpose of having money was to help those who are less fortunate.

I look at the older Kirk. "Yeah, when did you make that discovery?" I ask him, but he doesn't answer.

Young Kirk dissolved into old Kirk at a propitious time. He broke the blacklist during the McCarthy era. Many people warned him not to do it, but the daring of the younger Kirk met with the developing wisdom of the older Kirk and together they made it happen. The younger Kirk by himself would have been too self-protective to do it. The older Kirk alone would have been too conservative to try it.

Two heads are better than one. "Don't you agree?" I ask them.

Young Kirk just keeps grinning.

"By joining together," I say, "you helped me do the thing that I'm most proud of, putting an end to the blacklist by placing Dalton Trumbo's name as the writer of *Spartacus* instead of the pseudonym Sam Jackson."

Now, in the morning sunlight, the heads, forged from stainless steel, seem to sparkle. I look down at their shimmering reflections in the pool. The lips of the two Kirks, the young and the old, seem to be moving rapidly, both heads talking at once. I look up and they are silent, as if they don't want me to catch them gossiping.

I stare at the face of the young Kirk, fresh from World War II. He is smiling, all of his teeth showing. His unlined face is full of confidence. After I graduated from midshipman school at Notre Dame, I married Diana Dill, whom I had met at drama school in New York. We were married in New Orleans, a navy wedding. Long before Katrina, we marched down the aisle under crossed swords.

We lived in the Pontalba building, a famous architectural landmark on Jackson Square. Many years later, that is where President Bush spoke to the people of New Orleans.

I think lots of people got married when they entered the war because of a fear that they might die. Diana became the mother of my two older sons, Michael and Joel, but after Joel was born, she and I realized that we were not right for each other, and we divorced amicably.

This is how I remembered Kirk in my first book, *The Ragman's Son,* as a young naval officer, a newly married man going off to fight the war:

We sailed peacefully down the Mississippi, en route to Miami to pick up some radar gear before joining the war. I was being very gung ho, terribly official, and had the four sailors under me, my communications group, come into the wardroom so I could explain to them how I intended to run the department. As I was talking, the movement of the ship altered. It started to go up. And down. And up. And down. And I began to get a queasy feeling in my stomach. I ignored it for as long as I could and continued explaining codes. But the queasy feeling kept mounting, mounting, and suddenly I bolted out of the wardroom, ran to the side of the ship and threw up. I was the first one on the ship to be seasick. We had not yet entered the Gulf of Mexico.

"You remember, laughing boy?" I ask him. "Nah . . . all you remember is that German stewardess, a big, tall blonde. While you were having sex she would scream, 'I'm a Nazi!' and that was your cue to slap her, and you did. Remember? Well, I remember. Remember going through the Panama Canal with a short stop at the Galapagos Islands before sailing into the Pacific to look for Japanese submarines? Remember?" My God, that was sixty years ago.

Young Kirk still has that silly smile. I tell him, "Your first encounter with a Japanese submarine was a disaster." For us, not for them. A depth charge we released at the wrong time almost blew up our ship. We limped into Mexico, where I caught a serious case of amoebic dysentery and ended up in the San Diego Naval Hospital. "Remember?" I ask him, a bit more harshly. Nothing can erase that grin from his face. But I survived and we won the war.

I amble back to my seat. My coffee is cold.

I lean back, close my eyes, and continue to reminisce.

After the war, the United States became generous. With the Marshall Plan, we even helped our former enemies. We were the most popular country on the planet. How times have changed!

Then, everyone believed in the promise of the world getting better, progressing and evolving in a way that would benefit all of us. We expected everything to improve: health care, peace among nations, tolerance among people, technology, transportation, communication — everything. . . .

I look across the pool and study the two-headed Kirk as my two dogs study me. Danny is a yellow lab and Foxy is chocolate. Danny's name is really Danielovitch, my family name. He is a Jewish dog, but he doesn't know it. Foxy has lost one eye and the other eye is weak. He uses Danny as his seeing-eye dog. As usual, they are lying down on either side of me. I take a sip, forgetting that the coffee is cold.

Here I am, at the other end of that postwar promise, and I wonder: what the hell happened? It seems to be a question without an answer. Sure, things have improved a bit here and there. Some things have improved a whole lot. Other things are worse than ever before. But if I look at modern society with a view toward future generations, I have to ask myself, what kind of world am I leaving to my grandchildren?

What will happen to each of them? What kind of lives will they lead? Will they love, will they marry, will they have families of their own? Where will they go, what kind of work will they choose? Who will they be? What kind of world will we leave them?

Let's face it, the world is in a mess. I become irritable and walk around the pool to exercise my legs. My dogs follow and stop with me at the bust. The steel gives the bust such strength. A world of wisdom separates the two images, but I don't find any answers.

I look at the older Kirk, serene and too dignified.

My gaze shifts to the younger Kirk. He's still smiling, all his teeth showing. Those teeth did a lot of work in movies. "You remember puking, don't you? Ahh . . . all you remember is fucking."

He remains imperturbable. He was always such a cocky guy. Not the most likable actor in Hollywood. A lot of his colleagues wanted to kick his ass.

I'm too rough on young Kirk. I actually really like him. He's got a lot of spark — too much nerve, but he's never dull. Now I look at the old man — a real old fart. He's getting older, but is he any wiser? Look at him, he looks like a CEO who robbed the shareholders.

The two of them make quite a pair. I must get over the habit of talking to them, though. I really don't know why I do it.

My wife calls out, "Honey, I'm ready."

I hurry to the kitchen. Danny and Foxy follow, jostling for attention. I love my two dogs; their affection is endless. I give them each a cookie, leave them, and join my wife.

3
A DAY IN MY LIFE

Anne and I always start the day off with a workout at Mike Abrums's gym. Anne drives. She doesn't trust me. I remember a few years ago reaching into the side car-pocket for a bottle of water. I tried to rip off the plastic cap but I couldn't. I worried, *Did my stroke do so much damage?* Anne took the bottle and, with her arms guiding the steering wheel, she twisted off the cap and gave me the water. I was stunned but said nothing. Anne just looked ahead with a slight smirk. It was the first time she did something like that but not the last.

We have been working out with Mike for more than forty years. I don't know how much it's helped me, but it certainly has helped him. Mike is a tough ex-Marine, ninety-two years old, in perfect condition. I think Mike was the first one to advocate that you don't have to sweat to have a workout. He doesn't believe in "No pain, no gain." For years he preached moderation.

The gym is a large room with a twenty-foot-high ceiling. During my first exercise — sit-ups — I get my first laugh of the day. I look up, and hanging from the ceiling on a five-foot chain is a little black box painted with white letters that say "Suggestion Box." No one has ever been able to get up there to make a suggestion.

The whole workout routine takes twenty minutes and we do one routine after the other. It seems to work, especially for Mike. He goes salsa dancing three times a week until two in the morning. I don't go salsa dancing, and I'm younger than he is. I look at Anne gracefully doing her routine and decide to do more repetitions with my weights. Now, almost strong enough to rip off a bottle cap, I start rounds with Anne.

Today we're visiting Kirk Douglas High School, a school for troubled students. I don't know why they chose me to name the school after, but I'm honored. After my first visit, a group of boys formed a rap group and wrote a song to me. They sang so loud and so fast I didn't catch any of the words. They sent me a copy of the words later.

Today, the first thing I see when I drive up is that the side of the building is painted with a movie camera on a tripod, spilling out a roll of film inscribed with my name.

In the school all the students are assembled in a group and they give me a rousing welcome. I give a short talk, encouraging them to continue with their schoolwork. I promise to continue awarding each graduate a five-hundred-dollar gift.

Driving back, I read a note one of the students handed me:

Kirk Douglas High School came to me during a very critical point in my life — a screw-up that resulted in my expulsion from my old high school. . . . When it came down to it, that high school, which will remain nameless, didn't care about my future. All they cared about was their reputation and everything else involved in the politics of running a school. I was an expendable "problem child" because of that one mistake of mine, and when I was kicked out, my morale was low and my contempt for public schooling was immense. However, that all changed because of that one little "options school" named after the legendary actor that is you.

I feel good, but it's only 11 a.m.

Before lunch we make a short visit to the Kirk Douglas Theatre near the MGM Studio in Culver City. Over the years I've gone to Culver City many, many times while working at MGM. Some of my films were very good, like *The Bad and the Beautiful* and *Lust for Life.* I won't list the films I didn't like — there are too many. The new Kirk Douglas Theatre, which is dedicated to aspiring playwrights and actors, has lined up six plays for the season.

On the theater's opening night I gave a little talk. I told them that I felt like a failure. All of my life I yearned to be a star on the stage. In my old age, I found out how to do that: build your own theater!

So far the productions have been very well received. We now have a Thursday morning show for high school students. I'm arranging for students from the Kirk Douglas High School to see one of the productions. If it works out well, they may become regular customers.

Then we visit the grave of our son. We do it twice a week. It comforts us. He died in 2004 from a drug overdose. We sit on a little stone bench at the side of his grave and look at the slab of marble leaning against a small wall that bears his name:

Eric
1958–2004
DOUGLAS

I stare at the empty space that will some-day be engraved: KIRK–ANNE. My wife rakes the leaves on the small plot with her hands. Frankly, I like the rust-colored leaves resting on top of Eric, but my wife is very meticulous and soon the leaves are removed from the grassy patch and put in a plastic bag.

I think of the time Eric returned home for a visit after spending six months at the Institute of Living in Connecticut. He was then about thirteen years old, and doctors had advised us to send him there for anger management. I felt awkward. I asked him what he would like to do.

"I want to ride the pony in the park."

"Eric, you're too big for that."

"No, no, that's what I would like to do."

I gave in and watched him mount the small pony. He was much too big; the other riders were all about five or six years old. I watched Eric, legs dangling, slowly riding the pony around the ring. There was a smile on his face. He seemed so peaceful and serene. He didn't want to give up his childhood.

4
Hoops of Steel

I am writing in what I call my den. I like this room. It's my bedroom, my library, my workroom, my haven.

My wife's room is right next door. I subscribe to what the poet Kahlil Gibran said: "Let there be spaces in your togetherness." My wife agrees.

I look around my den. I like my space. One wall is covered with the Chagall *Bible Series,* painted in his almost childlike style with vivid colors. He's my favorite painter. Anne and I met him at the beach in the south of France. Anne asked him to autograph a Chagall book that had one of his paintings in the middle of a page. He took the book home and brought it back the next morning. He had extended the copy of the painting to fill the entire page and signed it to me. It hangs on my wall near the bookshelf.

Quietly, I get up and slowly open Anne's

door a crack. The room is dark; she is still sleeping. I softly close the door and retreat to my den. At my desk I open my computer to play a game of spider solitaire. I really don't know anything about computers, but my wife taught me to play this one game. Then I started playing it all the time on her computer. She became annoyed with me hogging her computer and bought me my own. I've become addicted to spider solitaire.

After I lose a few games, which always irritates me, I turn off the computer and look at a beautiful nude young woman standing in the middle of the rose garden. She is a life-size sculpture that I bought in Yugoslavia. How many years have we looked at each other through my den window? In the sunlight she looks beautiful. Yes, nude girl, you will be forever young.

I swing my chair around and face a wall covered with books, hundreds of them, all personally autographed. The top shelf holds my movie scripts. Bound in black leather, they look like little coffins. I wrote a comment in every one of them. I reach up and pull out my first script, *The Strange Love of Martha Ivers,* with its scratched-up cover. I smile at the memories and open up the script to see what I wrote: "My first film!

Lauren Bacall got the producer to see me in a play in New York. He gave me the part! Van Heflin was very helpful. Barbara Stanwyck ignored me for two weeks. Then she seemed to look at me for the first time and said, 'You're a good actor.' I said, 'Too late, Miss Stanwyck.' " But she and I became good friends.

Bacall is to blame for getting me into movies. She never should have talked to that producer. I might have fulfilled my ambition to be a star on the stage. I put the script back and take down *The Champion*. What did I write in this one? "My agent fought me not to do this film. What the hell do they know? It made me a star!" I must have been a difficult actor in those days.

My eyes go down the row of scripts, almost ninety of them — it looks endless. I reach out for another, *The Bad and the Beautiful.* Oh, I know what I wrote in this one. "I shot this while fasting on Yom Kippur. You try making love to Lana Turner on an empty stomach." That makes me laugh out loud. Lana Turner did her best acting in this picture. She was beautiful. Hollywood expected that something would happen when I teamed up with Lana. I was ready, but her boyfriend Fernando Lamas was always on the set.

I pull down another script, *Cast a Giant Shadow.* What did I say in it? "What fun shooting in Israel! Too many stars, Yul Brynner, Frank Sinatra, John Wayne, and me. John Wayne got me involved in this." Yes, I remember being in London and Wayne called me from Hollywood: "Kirk, I've got a wonderful script. You play the lead, I will play the small part of an American general." It always seemed curious to me that John Wayne was the catalyst for putting this picture together. My son Joel was there and he liked being my bodyguard. Michael was dressed in an Israeli army uniform and we used him in the shots of jeeps climbing the rugged mountain terrain. Michael is an excellent driver.

I pull down another book, *Seven Days in May,* and am startled to see what I wrote in 1995, at the time of the Oklahoma City bombing: "This movie should be reissued today when we are close to a revolution."

At random, I take down the 1964 script for *In Harm's Way.* Here is what I scribbled: "Another movie with Wayne. I got mad at MKD [my son Michael] and didn't let him come to Hawaii." I think I caught him smoking pot.

I put the script back. I did four movies

with Wayne. We were a strange combination. He was a Republican and I was a Democrat. We argued all the time. But after his death, his son Michael told me something I'll never forget: "My father always loved you, Kirk."

Enough of the past, let's move on to the future. I sit down at my desk and get to work on this book. Yet I keep looking up at the row of scripts — so many movies, so many friends I've worked with: Burt Lancaster, Walter Matthau, Rock Hudson, Lana Turner, Laurence Olivier, Ava Gardner, Frank Sinatra, and so many, many others, all gone.

When will I join them?

"Friend" seems to be a small, superficial word until you get older. Then friendship takes on a deeper meaning as you lose your friends to death. Shakespeare wrote the play *Hamlet* when he was thirty-eight years old. Even at that young age, however, he knew the value of friends:

Those friends thou hast, and their adoption tried,
Grapple them to thy soul with hoops of steel;
But do not dull thy palm with entertainment
Of each new-hatch'd, unfledg'd comrade.

As you get older, friendships become more important and memories more precious. Don't take true friends for granted. "Grapple them to thy soul with hoops of steel." Appreciate them before it's too late.

How can I ever forget my friend Burt Lancaster? We shared so many wonderful times. In London we did a song-and-dance routine for a charity benefit. Wearing bowler hats, wielding tightly wrapped umbrellas, and with terrible English accents, we sang, "Maybe It's Because I'm a Londoner That I Love London So." Then I climbed up on Burt's shoulders as we went off waving to the audience. They loved it. A picture of us rehearsing the skit now hangs on my dressing room wall and it makes me laugh every time I look at it.

This reminds me of a night I was being honored at a dinner. Burt Lancaster introduced me: "Kirk would be the *first* to admit he's a difficult person — [pause] . . . I would be the *second!*" We ribbed each other constantly. And then he had a stroke. His wife asked me to accept the SAG award for him, but she never let me visit. She thought it would depress him. He died and I never got the chance to say good-bye. Maybe now he's waiting for me to say hello.

Memories have a way of keeping you alive.

Frank and Barbara Sinatra were great hosts.
Every other Sunday they had a poker game,
very low stakes. The group usually consisted
of Mr. and Mrs. Gregory Peck, Mr. and
Mrs. Jack Lemmon, and Anne and me. After
Frank died, the game went on. When Greg-
ory Peck died, the game continued. Jack
Lemmon died, and it still continues.

The other day we played and all the
widows were there. I looked across the table
at my wife and thought, When I die, this
game will still go on, and they'll call it
widow's poker.

The memories of those friendly games
always make me smile.

The brain is such a wonderful thing — it
sorts out memories and you can relive them.
You open it up like a filing cabinet and pick
out the ones you like. You can hide the ones
that you are ashamed of or those that make
you unhappy.

I relish all the memories I have with my
wife, Anne, in Europe. I can still see her
rowing the boat in Amalfi, Italy, before we
were married. I am lying down, singing an
Italian song, "Come bello far l'amore
cuando è sera" — (Oh how lovely it is to

make love in the evening).

Some memories are poignant but they stay with you. One of mine is from 1945, several days after the death of Franklin Delano Roosevelt. On an early Sunday morning, few people were on the streets of Greenwich Village, where I lived at that time. I was walking toward the subway near Washington Square to get to Schrafft's, a restaurant on 82nd Street, where I worked as a waiter.

I spotted a woman walking alone. She looked familiar and I stopped and studied her. I was stunned. It was Eleanor Roosevelt, the wife of our president. I was tongue-tied as she passed me, but I managed to mutter, "Good morning, Mrs. Roosevelt." She looked at me with a toothy smile and answered, "Good morning," as she continued walking. I felt stupid. I wanted to run after her to express how sorry I felt about the death of our president, but I couldn't move. I just stood there and watched that dignified lady walking away.

Then there are Hollywood memories. How could I forget Yul Brynner sitting on the floor of our house in Palm Springs, strumming his guitar and singing sad old Russian folk songs in a rich baritone? He usually stayed with Frank Sinatra, but this time they'd had an argument so we adopted him for a few days until he made up with Frank.

Another memory makes me laugh. I gave Walter Matthau his first movie role in *The Indian Fighter.* He hated his horse and always cursed at it in Yiddish. In my mind I hear Walter Matthau telling me jokes in perfect Yiddish. His command of the language was much better than mine.

Abe and Sam bump into each other on the street. Abe says, "Oh, Sam, I'm so sorry, I just heard about the fire."
Sam: "Shh . . . it's tomorrow."

It plays better in Yiddish.

When I came to Hollywood, my first wife, Diana, and I were invited to a dinner. When it was over, everyone left before we did except Judy Garland and her friend, a pianist. Judy felt like singing, and for an hour she sang just for us. The rainbow was never so beautiful.

Once after a dinner party, Gregory Peck and I drove Fred Astaire home. Fred lived in a colonial house that had a long porch with many pillars. When we dropped him off, he danced along the whole front porch, then opened the door, tipped his hat to us, and disappeared.

Wow! Greg and I couldn't speak for a few minutes. It was a beautiful way to say thank you.

Memories can also be new.

I remember the moment when my wife — recently converted to Judaism — lit the candles and said the Hebrew prayers to welcome Shabbat. The candlesticks had been brought over from Russia by my mother; they had been given to Ma by her mother. They were well over a hundred years old.

I see my mother illuminated by candlelight while she says the prayers — I am nine years old. Now I have a memory of my wife doing the same thing — I am ninety.

I have a haunting memory that goes back eighty years. I am lying on a grassy river-bank under the shade of a eucalyptus tree. One hand is in the cool water as I listen to the muted cacophony of the town. I like it. I feel happy. Maybe that's what dying is like. Lying there at ten years old was the first time I felt engulfed by an invisible veil of melancholy, but not the last. Most of the time I'm not aware of it, but it's always there. When I think of the love my father never gave me I feel encased in a veil with steel threads. Remembrance of my mother's love changes my veil to gossamer threads. An anti-Semitic slur causes the veil to press against me. Sometimes a happy thought can make me jump for joy, but I must be careful; if I jump too high, I'll bump into the veil. It doesn't hurt, but it always tinges my joy with sadness.

Lucky is the person who has stored up many pleasant memories — he can risk jumping for joy.

5

AMSTERDAM, NEW YORK

When you achieve fame and more money than you ever dreamed of, it's easy to forget that you were once a poor Jewish boy without enough to eat.

And as you get older, your point of view changes. I look differently at many things that I have written in my books. For example, I wrote that my father left Russia to escape the pogroms. Now I realize he was also escaping a twenty-five-year term in the army. The Russian czar had instituted quotas for boys from every Jewish village to be sent into the army for twenty-five years. During that period they would be pressured to convert to Christianity.

Some Jews tried to escape that fate by cutting off their index fingers, which would keep them from being able to shoot a gun. Many Jews escaped from Russia during those years. One was Marc Chagall, who left Vitebsk in the area known as the Pale of

Settlement to make a name for himself in Paris. Czarina Catherine the Great had established the Pale of Settlement in 1791 as a territory for Russian Jews to live in. Created under pressure to rid Moscow of Jewish business competition and the "evil" Jewish influence on the Russian masses, the Pale of Settlement included the territories of present-day Latvia, Lithuania, Ukraine, and Belarus.

In 1910 Pa emigrated from a shtetl near Mogilev, south of Vitebsk, with his index finger intact. A handsome young Russian peasant, he came to the United States to seek his fortune. He had trouble supporting his family of six girls and one boy and he ended up in Amsterdam, New York, collecting rags and scrap metal in a wagon drawn by a white horse named Bill (he was really a gray horse but we always thought of him as white). Every morning my father went out into the town yelling for rags, paper, and scrap metal.

There was a section in the city called Cork Hill where no Jew except my father dared to go. He was the only Jew who plied his trade in Cork Hill. He was very strong and a fighter, and in Cork Hill when a gang would accost him, shouting "Kike" or "Jew bastard," Pa would pull up one of the wooden posts of the wagon and charge them. Finally, they left him alone.

My father's routine was to stop at the street corner on his way home, his wagon filled with rags and junk. He'd jump off the wagon and give the horse a slap on the rump, and Bill would trot back to our house, the last one on the street. My father would then trot to Bogie's saloon.

Bill usually pulled up by our door and stopped. I enjoyed unhitching him and leading him to the barn. I always got him a pail of water, which I could barely carry. He drank it greedily while we waited for my father to come home. It was a long wait.

The Cork Hill bullies got their revenge. Late one night, we were all awakened by the crackling of flames. Someone had set fire to our barn. Bill, who had so faithfully pulled my father's wagon all over Cork Hill and whom I loved, died in the fire.

If Pa had been born here or had come to this country as a boy instead of as a grown man with a family to support, I think he's the one who would have become an actor. Sometimes in the evening I prowled the alley behind the saloon and listened to my father regaling his friends with dramatic and comic stories. He could have been a wonderful actor. I think his disappointment with his lot kept him from showing the affection he really had for me.

My father gave me a good thrashing many times, but the moment I remember most was Pa standing in front of our dilapidated house as the rest of my family left him behind. My sisters insisted on moving to a better house. My father wanted to stay where we were. I looked at him. He stared at me but said nothing. I was thinking, "I'm the only boy in the family, why am I going with my sisters and mother? Seven women! Why am I leaving my father? Should I stay with him?" I was confused. I put my hands in my pockets and grabbed my crotch. I didn't want to be a girl. I wanted a father.

For years my father lived in the old house that we had left. I lived with my mother and my six sisters in a somewhat better house not far away. Having a nice home was important for my older sisters because young men came to call on them, but I felt uncomfortable and strange, always thinking of my father. One day, while walking home from school with some schoolmates, I saw my father in the wagon loaded with junk. I was embarrassed for a moment, then I ran into the street, hopped up on the wagon, climbed over the mound of junk, and sat with my father. We didn't say anything, and when we came to the corner of Eagle Street, he suggested that I jump off. I stood at the corner and watched my father going down the street in the wagon. I didn't know what to do so I went home to join my mother and sisters.

My thoughts at that time were all mixed up. I really didn't know what I was thinking, but I knew that I was sad. I decided to visit my father. I didn't know what to expect but I felt I had to see him. Pa was sitting in the kitchen cutting up a herring that he had bought. He offered me a piece. I ate it. I had so many things I wanted to say but I couldn't say anything. It was so dreary that I had to leave.

We never made contact with each other. If only he had said, "I love you — stay with me," I would have done so, but we didn't have the strength to say that to each other. It's so awful in life that many times we don't seize the opportunity to say something that should be said, to do something that should be done, and when we realize it, it's too late.

My first experience with sex was with my high school English teacher, Mrs. Livingston. The relationship was a turning point in my life. I had been a ragamuffin kid of fifteen coping with a neighborhood filled with gangs; under her guidance I became a different person. Mrs. Livingston taught me a love for poetry and literature, and she encouraged me to make an effort to go to college. She was an important influence in my life and I am eternally grateful. By today's standards she would have gone to jail. I had no idea we were doing something wrong. Did she?

Regardless, she inspired me with the excitement of learning. She even urged me to try to write a poem. This was my first attempt, "The Discarded Ship":

Above me have flown many flags
But now my sails are torn to rags
My bows are white from swirling foam
As o'er the many seas I roam
But now there's nothing left for me
I live in days that used to be.

I wrote that poem seventy-five years ago when I was fifteen years old. I had never seen the sea, and the longest journey I had ever taken from my hometown was to hitchhike to Schenectady, fifteen miles away. How could I have written that poem then? It's now that I feel like an abandoned ship. At the time, I enjoyed reciting my poem with feeling to Mrs. Livingston.

My next poem, in college, dealt with my immediate present. A beautiful young redhead sat in front of me in English class. Inspired by the passion of Shakespeare's sonnets, I made an attempt to woo her with verse:

How oft have I behind thee sat
In awe and watched thy titian hair
Resplendent in the rays
Of morning's golden light,
Dancing about thy head
For joy, a gorgeous sight!
Each ray thus shaped
A sparkling diadem
Of jewels to crown
You queen of beauty over all.
Bewitched by a vision so fair,
I reach out and touch your hair.
Happily you turn and smile at me
And change my humble state to ecstasy.

I got the girl. But you don't have to write bad poetry to get a good education. Or to sleep with your teacher.

When my mother died, I was at her bedside holding her hand. She was trying to comfort me until she exhaled her last breath. She said, "Death comes to everyone."

Years later when my father was dying I went to visit him, stayed a short time, and told him I had to go. When he asked me to stay longer, I answered, "Pa, you had your kids and now I have mine. Michael and Joel are waiting for me in New York." I started to leave, and these were the last words I heard my father mutter, "I will never see you again."

I left. I was cruel. I was trying to hurt him because he never gave me a pat on the back. I mean, I wanted him to recognize me — to be proud of me. I wanted him to love me. I didn't want to be a mama's boy.

Years after his death, a friend told me, "Oh, how proud your father was of you. We took him to see you in *Champion*. And when you were losing the fight, your father got up and yelled, 'Hit him, Issur! Hit him!' "

Yes, but he never told me that. It was too late.

6
CHILDREN

It's a chilly morning. It rained all night and I don't want to get out of bed. I love the rain but I always feel a twinge of sadness at the image of rain beating down on Eric's lonely grave. I hear a soft knock on the door and Lettie, my housekeeper, comes in with my morning coffee. I call her Lettie, but her name is really Leticia. She is from the Philippines. She began living with and working for us six years ago. Not long after she started, she told us that she had a husband in the Philippines, Victor, who was not able to get a visa to come here. We thought it was awful for them to be separated, so my wife arranged to get him into the country. Lettie said that he'd be willing to sleep on the floor in her room. My wife was appalled. "Go out and get a king-size bed," she told Lettie, and Lettie did.

Then Victor, a very nice guy, needed a job. Anne found him one, and once again peace reigned in our household. Six months later, we received Lettie's news: "I'm pregnant." I thought their room would be too crowded for three, so I had one wall knocked down. Forty thousand dollars later the room was at least six feet wider and ready to receive the baby girl, Victoria. And a few years later Anne arranged for Victoria to attend a preschool not far from our house.

As I'm ruminating, the door opens and little Victoria, four years old, comes over to my bed and says, "Good morning, Pappy." (Like my grandchildren, she calls me Pappy. I made sure they would never call me Grandpa.) She gives me a quick kiss and hurries off for school. This is her usual routine. I like it.

I listen to her little feet running down the hallway. She never walks.

This book is for Cameron, Kelsey, Ryan, Tyler, Dylan, Carys, and Jason, my grandchildren. I want them to know more about Pappy. I want them to know how I see things at this point in my life — maybe it will help them avoid the mistakes I made.

I love all of you very much. I won't be around when most of you reach maturity, but I hope that you will find a belief in a higher power that will lead you to be good citizens and help others.

My grandchildren fascinate me, and I'm happy that they seem to have found ways to express themselves. Cameron, the oldest, has already played in several movies and shows the promise of being a good actor. Kelsey, at age thirteen, has a room full of first-prize ribbons in horsemanship. Ten-year-old Tyler is quiet, confident, and bright. Three years ago, we discovered that he had a natural talent for golf and now he can beat me. Ryan, five years old, is a very caring person. He watches out for his younger brother, Jason, who's two and races bowlegged around the house like a football player (he inherited the legs from me, along with a dimple in his chin).

Michael's two young children now live with their parents in Bermuda. At five, Dylan can swim like a fish. "Pappy," he calls out to me from the swimming pool, "throw something in the water." I throw a quarter. Dylan dives down, retrieves the quarter, bursts up to the surface, and shouts, "Da-da-da!" (He's also a ham.) Carys, his three-year-old sister, also shows talent. When they ask her to imitate Pappy, she grits her teeth and pushes her face forward.

■ ■ ■ ■

I love all children and I want them to get a good education from good teachers. Our education system is far from what it should be. Many schools around the world are ahead of us, especially in math and science. Washington doesn't spend enough money to improve our schools and teachers. Is that because children don't vote?

7
MY SONS

The problems of the world have changed so much from the days when I was young. In the 1940s we thought of wars being fought thousands of miles away. Of course we were astounded by Pearl Harbor, but even that was far away in Hawaii. The lives my sons and grandchildren lead are so different from my life.

In my generation, especially if your parents were foreign born, you worked and took care of your father and mother in their old age. Now we live in a different era. Baby boomers are supported by trust funds from their parents.

I've told my sons that they missed out on a lot because they were not born poor. How about the experience of the wind whipping your face as you hitchhike a ride on top of a load of fertilizer on your way to college? And they will never know what it's like to be hungry in New York on Thanksgiving

Day. I once walked to the Bowery to get in line at the Salvation Army center for a Thanksgiving dinner. The line was long, and when I finally got to the window they were out of dinners.

I was already down; I had nowhere to go but up. I do think that you have more of an incentive to achieve your goals in life when you're born poor.

In ancient times, people always knew who was the mother of a child, but they were not sure of the father. Thus according to Jewish law, to be Jewish you had to have a Jewish mother. This idea goes back to Abraham, who had two sons — Isaac and Ishmael. Isaac, the son of his Hebrew wife, Sarah, became the progenitor of the Jews, while Ishmael, the son of his Egyptian wife, Hagar, became the progenitor of the Arabs. I have been married twice, both times to non-Jewish women. I had two sons with each wife. None of my sons could be Jewish unless they converted. But they all know that I am a Jew, even though I never taught them any Torah law.

My son Michael is a good father. His son Cameron, twenty-seven, played in a movie, *It Runs in the Family,* starring Michael and me. (It certainly does run in the family.) Then he did *Adam and Eve,* a movie directed by Jeff Kanew.

I wonder if Cameron ever heard the story of what happened to his father in prep school because he was half-Jewish. A big bully at Choate kept taunting Michael, "Half-breed!" and pushing him. One day Michael turned away, whirled around, and hit the bully with his fist flush on the face. All taunts stopped.

Several times I complained to Michael that he never asked me for anything. I still have the card he wrote on my eighty-second birthday:

Dad,
You say I never ask you for anything but you give me a lot.

Love, Michael

The card was on the steering wheel of a new car, my present.

To celebrate my eighty-sixth year, Michael arranged to have eighty-six trees planted in Israel in my honor. From the beginning, Jews have always contributed money to plant trees in that arid desert land. My son doesn't have to be a Jew to give me such a wonderful birthday present. Michael is a caring person who believes in God and does much for other people. That's enough for me.

Joel has the best sense of humor of all my sons. Years ago, I had dinner with Joel in a restaurant and when the bill arrived I paid in cash. Joel said, "Dad, don't use money — just give him your autograph."

One summer we were shooting a film on location. My wife, Anne, got locked in the trailer lavatory. She pounded on the door inside, and I tried to open the door from the outside. Joel shouted, "Everybody get away from the door!" And he smashed the door in with one kick.

Joel is married to a fine woman, Jo Ann. They both go to a Catholic church every Sunday. I approve of that.

My third son, Peter, loves animals. During his youth he had many of them: a rabbit, a turtle, a ferret, a twelve-foot-long snake, and a cat named Bosco. Peter could yell out the window, "Bosco!" and the cat would come running back. I still marvel at that. You can call a dog to come — but rarely a cat!

As he got older, Peter's interests shifted to photography. When he was seventeen, I heard some activity at the pool early one morning. I looked out the window and saw Peter taking pictures of a nude girl standing on the diving board with his snake draped around her neck.

Peter is the tallest in the family, six foot two, and handsome, with curly hair. I once told him, "When I was starting out, I wanted to be six two instead of five eleven. I wanted to have curly hair, not straight hair. Why didn't you become an actor?"

Peter answered, "And compete against you and Michael? No way!"

My youngest son, Eric, was the shortest in the family, with straight hair. He wanted to be an actor. He tried very hard, but drugs came into his life.

8
ERIC

Eric had problems all his life. Was I one of his problems? People in the public eye often neglect their home lives. I was no exception.

Eric was a bright, towheaded boy with a ready smile who always wanted his own way. We once had a talk with the principal of his school. He pointed out the window to a track around a field of green grass and said, "Whenever I see a class running around the track and one boy is running on the grass, I know it's Eric."

In his youth Eric was very different from the man he grew up to be. If he was reprimanded and sent to his room, he seemed glad. He would pick up a book and start reading it, and we could hear him humming a song.

Yet he had rapid mood changes. One night I came home from the studio to find my wife, Anne, upset. During a talk she'd had with Eric, he became enraged and punched her in the stomach. This infuriated me. I found Eric, then nine years old, threw him over my lap, and gave him a spanking. Michael was watching. Years later, we discussed the incident.

Michael said, "Dad, you were guilty of child abuse."

I was stunned. "How can you say that?" I asked.

His answer was, "Whenever you strike a child in anger, that's child abuse."

I had no reply.

When Eric was twelve years old, I traveled cross-country with him to the Institute of Living, an establishment in Connecticut that had been highly recommended to help him manage his anger. This was the first of many places that we hoped would help Eric.

I filled out his application, then the doctor led him by the hand down a long hall. As I watched, he seemed like such a small boy, holding the hand of the tall doctor. Eric turned to me with a perplexed look on his face. I couldn't stop crying. The institute didn't help him very much. In fact, it aggravated his problem: he was sexually assaulted by two older patients.

Nevertheless, he graduated from Claremont College and made some movies and

TV shows. He worked in England, Russia, and France. He had his mother's talent for languages. After one month in France he spoke French. After a few months in Germany, he got by in German.

He tried too hard to compete with his father and oldest brother, though. For a time, he worked as a stand-up comic. In his act, he held up a big picture of the three of us — Michael, me, and himself. Eric pointed to each photo in succession and said, "Michael — Oscar winner, Kirk — Oscar winner, Eric — Oscar wiener." Big laugh.

It made me feel sad.

I did a TV show, "Yellow," with him for HBO, part of the *Tales from the Crypt* series directed by Robert Zemeckis. Dan Aykroyd was in the cast, but Eric played the lead. He was very good.

Eric was always difficult to handle. We consulted doctors and psychiatrists. Were we doing something wrong? The best advice we were given was: "You can only love and give and do the best according to your ability, but you cannot do the impossible. Accept what you cannot change."

That helped us to accept Eric, but it didn't seem to help him.

I don't know when alcohol and drugs became his problem. He went to many rehabilitation centers — Hazelden, the Betty Ford Center, the Menninger Clinic, Beacon House, Thalians, Columbia Presbyterian Hospital, and many others — over a twenty-year period. We attended meetings at the rehabilitation centers and talked with the counselors and psychologists. Nothing helped.

Anne and I finally learned that Eric had to *want* to get well. He had to admit that he was an addict and ask a higher power for help. At one of the rehabilitation centers, he became a Jew and was bar mitzvahed. That surprised me. Did he do that to please me? I don't know.

We often talked together about his problems. Yet somehow, we didn't talk about his bar mitzvah. I think that was my fault. I felt guilty because I hadn't attended.

My wife invited Eric to a meeting at the Anne Douglas Center for Homeless Women, a place for women with drug problems. Anne allowed Eric to participate in the meeting. He got up and spoke and he was wonderful. He admitted he was a drug addict and was planning to break the habit. He told others how they could overcome their addictions. The group was enthusiastic and responsive to Eric.

He could help other people, but he couldn't help himself. He had been close to death several times, but we had always been able to save him. One evening he had dinner with us. We had a very pleasant time and Eric seemed happy. He was charming and amusing. Anne and I were pleased; we thought he was on the right track. He went to sleep in the guesthouse.

Or rather, we thought he'd gone to sleep. We didn't know that he'd climbed over the fence to get drugs and alcohol.

The next morning, I had breakfast with him. He showed no sign of his night's binge. Suddenly, he keeled over, unconscious. We gave him mouth-to-mouth resuscitation and called an ambulance. He was in a coma at the hospital for several days. He came out of it and was the same old Eric, traveling from one rehabilitation center to another.

I tried to get him involved in forming a facility to help others. I offered to support it. He was not interested.

Anne is a very controlled person, but one day I came home to find her sobbing wildly. "I killed him, I killed him," she said. Eric had just died from an overdose in his New York apartment. Anne's first reaction was guilt. "It's all my fault," she said. I felt it was *my* fault.

No matter how much you think about such an event, you are never really prepared. It broke my heart that my son Eric died at forty-five and I'm still alive. I feel guilty that my youngest son lived a life of pain and died before I did. He didn't have a chance to taste the sweetness of life. He didn't get to fall in love, get married, and have children. Is it my fault? Did I somehow cause him to choose this path? My wife and I discuss it. We know that for years and years we tried to do everything we could.

Too many things are out of your control.

We brought Eric's body back to Beverly Hills. At the funeral, all of his brothers spoke. It was painful to bury our youngest son in the family plot.

I will never forget the sound of my shovelful of earth falling on his casket.

9
DEALING WITH DEATH

During our two visits a week to the cemetery, Anne and I sit on the stone bench next to his grave and talk to our son. It helps us.

"Eric, I brought this little silver cup. Remember? You gave it to me on my birthday ten years ago. Let me read what you had inscribed."

Dad — From the time of *your* birth, "Issur,"
Remember who you are, what you've done,
And the opportunities that await . . .
As your youngest child I thank you so much
For being there from *my* birth.
Love, Eric

12.09.96

I tell him, "Eric, I hope you have found peace. Your life was so painful. Someday, I will be buried beside you."

After his death, we received many letters of condolence. Many people wrote of similar experiences in their families about disturbed children whom they didn't know how to handle. It is tragic. We sought help in dealing with Eric's problem and we were constantly reassured that we could do no more to help him. The professionals gave us the three Cs:

We didn't *cause* it.
We can't *cure* it.
We can't *control* it.

Believe me, those professional prescriptions don't help when your son dies. Friends do.

Mona, Karl Malden's wife, tried to comfort us with a quotation from J. M. Barrie: "One who died is only a little ahead of the procession, all moving that way. When we round the corner we'll see him again. We have only lost him for a moment, because we fell behind stopping to tie a shoe-lace."

Jennifer Jones had a daughter who committed suicide at the age of twenty-one. Jennifer wrote, "I well know how parents must grieve for a lost child. I have been through that myself and can feel your pain just as if it were mine too. So as you mourn, I will also mourn; as you feel the loss, I will feel it too. You are my beloved friends, so I will join you in weeping for the lost one."

I wish Eric could have read this one: "Eric was, I believe, one of the most talented actors I have ever known. . . . His work on the *Tales from the Crypt* with his father was just amazing. Imagine, he stole the show from Kirk Douglas!" I never found out who sent it.

There were hundreds of others. Their words were like a healing salve on a wound, but I still felt guilt. After I survived a midair crash between our helicopter and a small plane, I felt guilty. Two young people had died, and I — in my seventies then — was still alive. Why? Imagine my guilt at the death of my son, who was half my age.

Was it suicide? I will never know.

I sit at my desk looking at my last book, *My Stroke of Luck*. In it I dealt with the suicidal impulse caused by my inability to speak. At the time I tried to joke, "What can an actor who can't talk do — wait for silent pictures to come back?" But it wasn't funny. My depression grew until I found myself with a gun in my hand. What stopped me was the realization that suicide is a selfish act. You're only thinking of yourself, not of the people you will leave behind.

During my convalescence, I learned to deal with depression. The best antidote is to think of others. Depression is caused by dwelling on your own woes. I had to realize that things could always be worse. Yet I was an old man with many years of living behind me. How does a young person, thinking of suicide, deal with depression? It is very difficult to understand.

The FDA finds antidepressants dangerous for teenagers. Too many doctors are too quick to provide pills. In his youth, we never gave Eric any antidepressants, but in his teens Eric had no trouble getting all the pills he wanted, in Los Angeles or New York. We filed a complaint against a doctor who prescribed drugs freely for him — this doctor lost his license and now faces jail. But there were other doctors eager to take his place.

Sitting on the stone bench at Eric's grave, I thought about how hard it is for kids to grow up in Hollywood. Maybe the fame of their parents or siblings is too much to handle. So many of these young people have tried to solve their problems by committing suicide or taking drugs, which resulted in their deaths.

Gregory Peck's son, suicide
Louis Jourdan's son, suicide
Carroll O'Connor's son, overdose
Ray Stark's son, suicide
Tony Curtis's son, overdose
Paul Newman's son, overdose
Barbara Eden's son, overdose
Marlon Brando's daughter, suicide
Walter Winchell's son, suicide
Chuck Barris's daughter, overdose
Charles Boyer's son, suicide
Bing Crosby's two sons, both suicide
Danielle Steel's son, overdose
Joss Ackland's son, overdose
Ian Fleming's son, overdose
Chuck Hearn's son, overdose
Jill Ireland's son, overdose
Boz Scaggs's son, overdose
Ethel Merman's daughter, overdose
Cloris Leachman's son, overdose
Ursula Thiess's son, overdose
And on and on it goes.

I get up to leave the cemetery and look once more at Eric's name. Then I turn around and leave, feeling guilty that Eric is all alone.

10
HARRY'S HAVEN

When I became successful in my career, I started my own production company, which I named Bryna, after my mother. Years later I took over the Alzheimer's unit at the Motion Picture & Television Home and decided to call it Harry's Haven, after my father, who never had Alzheimer's. Some of my friends asked me, "Why Harry's Haven? It sounds like a saloon." My answer: "Pa would like that. He spent a lot of time in saloons." I thought that with Harry's Haven, it was time to give my father the recognition he never gave me.

I supported my mother and father until their deaths. I also helped my six sisters, and I still help the two who are living. I didn't do this because I'm a nice guy. I did it because I owed it to them, because they all permitted me to get away — to college and drama school and eventually to find a career.

I visit Harry's Haven periodically. Each resident has a private room with his or her first name on the door in large letters and a picture. I didn't take over Harry's Haven just for the Alzheimer's patients — my aim is to help their families as well. How awful it must be to live with a loved one who doesn't know who you are.

Here, they are well taken care of, they have a nice garden for strolling, and every plant is edible. The patients seem to have a compulsion to reach out and chew on the plants. Families can visit whenever they want.

One Thanksgiving Day, I read an article on the front page of the *New York Times*. A forty-nine-year-old career woman had quit her job as a successful radio news anchor to go back to her childhood home to take care of her father, who had Alzheimer's. How sad! Many women and men are leaving their careers because they feel a need to go home to take care of sick parents.

Yet I can understand a spouse choosing to live with an afflicted husband or wife. When President Reagan announced to the public that he had Alzheimer's, his wife, Nancy, insisted on living with him. I admire her for that.

Nancy always took care of Ronnie. When

they invited us to dinner parties, she arranged for Anne to sit next to Ronnie because Anne has very good hearing but the president didn't.

One time, Anne was sitting between President Reagan and Bob Hope. Both of those guys had hearing problems. Whenever the president wanted to tell Bob a joke, he would tell it to Anne first and then she would repeat it to Bob. Then Bob would do the same thing. Finally the president told Anne a dirty joke and she refused to tell it to Bob. Ronnie burst out laughing.

11

DON'T PUT YOUR DAUGHTER (OR SON) ON THE STAGE!

This is the title of a song written by Noel Coward. On his visit to Los Angeles all the stars in Hollywood looked up to him as if he were a *real* star high above the firmament. At a dinner in his honor he sat at the piano and sang this hilarious song. It also makes sense.

I established the Kirk Douglas Theatre primarily to give young actors, young playwrights, and young directors a chance. I've been pleased by the young talent that I've seen on the stage. But I've never encouraged anyone, including my four sons, to enter the world of entertainment. As a matter of fact, I discouraged them. But who listens to me?

I feel sorry for actors. We are so vulnerable. Our product is ourselves. Adverse criticism is hard to take. The chances of an actor succeeding are few. You might know of hundreds of actors, but there are untold thousands of them that you've never heard of. People should pursue the acting profession only if they are compelled to and are willing to take the risk.

Actors pay a penalty whether they succeed or fail. Of course, a failed actor has a hard time surviving economically. Most often he is forced to take another job while he waits and waits and waits. In any restaurant in L.A., when I'm being served by a nice-looking boy or girl, I ask, "Are you an actor?" Their answer is almost always yes.

A successful actor who becomes a star loses all privacy. That can be a harder burden than you'd think. The actor is then pursued by paparazzi and besieged by organizations wanting his help. Marriages between famous actors rarely last.

When Michael went to college at the University of California at Santa Barbara, I thought he would study to be a lawyer and I was very pleased. Every Jewish parent wants to have a lawyer or a doctor in the family — or both. As the joke goes:

A Jewish mother is walking down the street with her two young sons. A passerby asks her how old the boys are.

"The doctor is three," the mother answers, "and the lawyer is two."

In his sophomore year, Michael told me he was going to be in a play. I was surprised, but I went to see him. He had a small part in Shakespeare's *As You Like It.* When the curtain finally fell Michael asked, "How was I, Dad?" "Awful," I answered. "I couldn't understand a word that Shakespeare had written for you." I was sure that would squelch any ideas he had about becoming an actor.

A few months later, he said, "Dad, I'm going to be in a play again." This guy never learns, I thought, but I went to see him. It was a two-character play. In his dressing room, Michael again asked, "How was I, Dad?" I surprised him with my answer. "You were very good," I said, honestly. And he's been very good in all the parts he's played since then.

I've seen Michael acting in arenas so small that the actors could spray you with spit while speaking. I've watched him in school plays, in church auditoriums, in summer stock, and, finally, on Broadway.

He auditioned for the lead in the play *Summertree* and he got the part. He was so happy during the rehearsal, but one day he came over to my hotel room (I was in New

York filming *The Brotherhood*) with a sad face.

"What happened?" I asked.

"Dad, they fired me."

"What!"

"They cast someone else to play my part."

His first rejection. Rejection is hard to take, especially for actors. It devastates you.

I ended up buying the rights to the play and I made it into a movie. Michael played the part that had been taken away from him, and he was very good.

I've spent most of my life portraying characters on stage or on screen and I'm still not sure of the answer to the question: what is an actor? I think that an actor is a man or a woman who has never completely lost his or her childishness. A sophisticated person might ask, "Kirk, you are a grown-up man. How can you pretend to be a cowboy shooting it out with Burt Lancaster? Aren't you embarrassed?"

No. An actor must be capable of retaining that quality of make-believe he had when he was a child. Watch children playing. They are wonderful, natural actors as they pretend to be other characters.

Many people become actors to escape reality. I think I was one of them. The problem actors must face is knowing when they are pretending to be other people and when they are themselves. When actors become stars, they often have trouble with their own identities. They are not prepared to be recognized everywhere and they are often confounded by the large amounts of money they earn. Then they begin to lose themselves, and pretending to be other people becomes easier for them.

Kabbalah teaches, "As a drop of water dissolves in the sea, so we are the ocean in the waves of nothingness — God." Kabbalists believe that God is nothing — no thing. And God created the world ex nihilo, "from nothing."

In some ways, artists imitate God. A composer sits at the piano or in his chair with his pen in his hand. From nothing, he creates music. A painter stands at his easel in front of a blank canvas, and from nothing, he creates a painting.

So it is with an actor. He must erase himself and become nothing in order to create another character.

Everything in life is a learning experience. Though emptying yourself is necessary in acting, you cannot remain empty — you have to fill that emptiness with something. I found that in acting I have learned about my limitations, how far I would go in certain circumstances. When acting, I inserted that bit of knowledge into the empty part of me.

Actors also need to study people, which helps them to be aware of others. An actor should try to ascertain another person's motivation for doing things that affect him, as well as his own motives. That helps him to become more compassionate.

You know, I made ninety movies. Only one of them, *Lust for Life,* demonstrates to me the process of erasing myself and becoming another character. I made the movie in 1956 and it wasn't released on DVD until 2006. Even at this late date, some critics reviewed it again. David Thomson called *Lust for Life* "as moving as anything in American cinema." Terry Teachout of the *Wall Street Journal* said, "It's both moving and convincing in its thoughtful portrayal of the Dutch painter, and Mr. Douglas, who in 1956 actually looked more than a little bit like van Gogh, gave one of the best performances of his long career." (You can't accuse me of modesty!)

Making the movie was painful for me. I don't know if it was a good example of a Stanislavsky or Actor's Studio method of acting, but I actually felt Vincent van Gogh's pain. One might say I was supposed to be creating the illusion of pain, letting the audience feel it. But when I portrayed Vincent he got the better of me. I erased myself and he took over. I made something from nothing. That movie's still too difficult for me to watch.

While making the movie in Holland I visited the Van Gogh Museum in Amsterdam, which has a room filled with the artist's self-portraits. I walked around and studied them. My hair and beard were tinted red like van Gogh's. I looked around and saw about a hundred visitors intently watching me.

Joaquin Phoenix excelled in the role of Johnny Cash in the 2005 picture *Walk the Line.* I felt great rapport with him as an actor when he said, "I had been desperate to disappear into a character completely." That's the epitome of good acting, and it doesn't happen often.

I knew Johnny Cash. We did a picture together that was not very successful, but to me the reward was meeting him. The last time I saw the man in black we were receiving the Presidential Medal of the Arts, given by President and Laura Bush. It was a memorable occasion. Yo-Yo Ma played the cello, accompanied by Condoleezza Rice on the piano. I nudged Johnny. "Are you going to sing?" He laughed. I miss that guy.

An actor lives many lives. I have been a cowboy (*Gunfight at the O.K. Corral*), a sailor (*20,000 Leagues under the Sea*), a soldier (*Paths of Glory*), a policeman (*Detective Story*), and an artist (*Lust for Life*). You just go from one life to another.

As I grow older I have less desire to erase myself and create another character. I have done that for so many years and with so many characters. I don't want to erase myself now. I want to delve within myself and see what I find.

How much time did I waste? I don't know, but now is the time to have an audit of my life. It's too bad that it took me so long to learn how to live. I thought I would live forever.

Wait, slow down a minute. I'm not prepared.

Let's face it, we must all learn how to deal with death.

12
FANS

In the early days of film, fans were not much of a nuisance. Sometimes they were even funny. I have often told this story. Years ago, I was hurrying to a luncheon date in Manhattan. I was stopped by a frantic fan in front of me yelling, "You're my favorite actor. I *love* you!"

I smiled and said, "Thank you" but didn't stop walking.

He kept pace with me, walking backward and yelling, "I'm so excited — your name just went out of my head!"

I tried to help him out. "Douglas."

"Yeah!" he shouted proudly, "Douglas Fairbanks, my *favorite* actor!"

That kind of thing keeps you from getting too smug. One night I was having dinner in a well-known restaurant where pictures of movie stars, mine included, cover the walls. A woman came over to me, holding a young child. She gushed, "Mr. Douglas, you remember that you took a picture holding my boy when he was eight months old?"

"Of course," I lied.

"He's three years old now," she said happily as she moved away.

Then a man came over and grabbed my hand. "Do you know what my favorite picture is?"

I hate questions like that. But he answered it for me: *Man without a Star.*

"Oh yes!" I lied again, trying to remember this movie that I made so long ago.

"That was my favorite," he added, squeezing my hand before he left. My dinner companions were very impressed by my popularity. I decided to lay it on even thicker. As a young busboy placed bread on my butter plate, I said, "Please say hello to the chef for me."

"Yes," he answered.

He stood there. I looked up at him.

"What's your name?" he asked.

I realized that there are millions of young people who have never seen any of my movies and don't know who the hell I am.

But that's better than the beautiful young girl with dewy eyes who once asked for my autograph. As I reached for my pen she said in awe, "Wow, Michael Douglas's father."

■ ■ ■ ■

Actors are often annoyed by fans. They stand outside restaurants with photos to autograph. Many fans do that just to sell the pictures. So many fans write letters asking me to autograph books and photos. I think it's wrong to use a stamp to do your job, so I always autograph them personally.

Some fans become too emotional. One English fan sent me poems that she had written to me. Then came a published book, *Poems for K.*

I have had a certain female fan for more than thirty years who never forgets a holiday, an anniversary, or a birthday. I always receive an affectionate note. In the past, she used to send me presents, until I was forced to write to her of my appreciation but implore her not to send me gifts (some of them were expensive). She heeded my request.

Many fans send me presents and pictures, but my favorite fan is the Lox Man, Saul Miller, who owns a delicatessen in New York. He sends me smoked salmon (lox) and smoked whitefish. I must write to him one of these days to say that he shouldn't send such expensive gifts, but his fish is so delicious.

Some fan letters are delightful. A lady sent me a copy of my book *My Stroke of Luck* to be autographed for her hundredth birthday. She had read the book twice and found it very helpful.

In my youth I never was a movie fan, but once I wrote a fan letter to Charles Laughton. It was 1939, the year I graduated from college and the year *The Hunchback of Notre Dame* was released. I was intrigued by Laughton's performance. In my fan letter I asked him questions about being an actor. He never answered. Years later we worked together in *Spartacus.* Watching him perform answered a lot of my questions.

Sixty-seven years later I wrote my second fan letter:

Dear Al Pacino,
Years ago, I sat in a little theater and watched a play, *The Indian Wants the Bronx,* written by Israel Horowitz, starring Al Pacino.

I was mesmerized by your performance, your ability to look directly into the audience and take command. It was long ago and maybe you've forgotten. I came backstage to pat you on the back and say that you will be a star.

I don't go to movie theaters very often but I watch you on TV. Every time I come across the title *Scent of a Woman* I can't resist. I must watch you play the scene of a blind man doing the tango and make it believable.

You are a good actor — a great actor.

All my best,
Kirk Douglas

This time I got an answer:

Dear Mr. Douglas,

The last time I was this thrilled to hear from someone was when you came and visited backstage at *The Indian Wants the Bronx.* It was a moment I will never forget. Now your letter to me has touched my heart. You are someone who has more than survived; you have conquered, very gently and very generously. Thanks for the gift of your note. I have admired you all these years, taking in your great work. I recently saw *Lonely Are the Brave* for the third time. It's a great film and your performance is something everyone should watch once a week for the rest of their lives.

Much love,
Al Pacino

Al Pacino is a part of a group of movie people I admire very much, including Robert DeNiro, Richard Dreyfuss, Martin Scorsese, and many others. I thought of them as the new actors until I saw Robert DeNiro's December 2006 interview with Larry King. Larry asked Robert his age, and he answered sixty-three. There must be younger actors who think *he's* an old-timer. What does that make me? A very, *very* old-timer.

One night, my wife and I attended a one-woman performance by Adriana Sevan at the Kirk Douglas Theatre. We watched her from the first row. She was very good. In the middle of her ninety-minute performance, she twisted her knee and fell to the floor in pain. At first, the audience thought it was part of the act. Then, over the loudspeaker, the stage manager asked the audience to convene in the lobby. As we left I walked onto the stage, kissed her on the forehead, and jokingly said, "I'm going to have a drink on you." That brought a smile to her face.

After a twenty-minute intermission in the lobby — and I did have my drink — we were able to go back to our seats. Adriana was in a chair with her left knee wrapped in ice. She did the rest of the show sitting there, and she was very good. The audience was very responsive, and afterward I went up to the stage again, put my arm around her, and said to her and the audience, "My wife and I are very glad that we drove back from Montecito to see your show, Adriana. For two reasons: first, because you're such a talented performer and second, because you have such courage."

A few days later, I received the most touching fan letter in my memory:

Dear Mr. Douglas,
May I begin by telling you what an honor and surprise it was for me to have you and your beautiful wife at my opening! As I was writhing on the floor in pain one of the producers whispered in my ear, "Mr. Douglas is here. . . ." And I flipped over to see you. For a moment all the pain went on pause and I had to catch my breath. It was really you!! . . . I felt like Dorothy waking from her dream but instead of the scarecrow and lion being around my bed . . . it was SPARTA-CUS!!!

I finished the play and was awed and humbled by the generous ovation, but nothing prepared me for the gift of your words. I could not believe that standing onstage next to me was Mr. Kirk Douglas. . . . For a moment I wondered if someone had given me acid instead of Advil! . . . Mr. Douglas, thank you for single-handedly making my opening night such a special night. And when I need to be reminded about what is lasting and important I will remember you and what you said.

When you reach ninety, you don't have to worry about being modest.

13
INSIDE OF ME

Throughout my life, locked up inside of me is always little Issur from Amsterdam, New York. I often forget that I'm a movie star. I forget the status that it brings, and I become a fan. One afternoon a few years ago, President Carter and his wife, Rosalynn, came to pay us a visit at our home. Sitting with them in the living room I was a fan — little Issur reminding himself that this was the president of the United States, visiting me. The Kirk Douglas who received the Medal of Freedom, the highest civilian award, from President Carter was someone else. It was difficult for me to handle the reality.

Over the years I've had many encounters with Henry Kissinger. He has come to several dinners at my home, he was a week-long guest at my Palm Springs house, and we went together to watch the takeoff of the first Apollo flight to the moon.

Recently, while I was in New York for discussions about this book with my publisher, I got a call from Henry asking whether he could stop by at my hotel for a visit.

Kirk Douglas could accept that, but little Issur inside me was very excited — the famous former secretary of state was coming to visit me! I couldn't believe it. During Henry's cordial visit I tried to make Kirk Douglas take over — but Issur was always there.

When I first met James Cagney — wow, was I a fan! I had worshiped him in *Yankee Doodle Dandy.* And then he startled me by saying a few words in Yiddish. He was an Irish boy who had been raised in a Jewish neighborhood.

Separating the reality of Kirk Douglas from the dreams of Issur remains something I haven't been able to accomplish. I think it's because I like Issur more than I like Kirk Douglas.

Sometimes, when I'm sitting out in the sun on my terrace in Montecito, I hear the far-off wail of a passing train. It makes me feel sad in a happy way (if you'll forgive my oxymoron). We lived near the railroad tracks when I was a boy, and the sounds of trains are very nostalgic to me. I could see them speeding past because the express train never stopped in our little town. Where were they hurrying to?

I can still see Issur leaning on the front fence in the evening and playing out scenes he had watched in the movies, concocting dreams of the future. As I got older, I found that the fulfillment of my dreams was not as exciting as when I first dreamed those dreams, leaning on a picket fence.

14
ROMANCE BEGINS AT EIGHTY

A sound awakens me and I open my eyes and listen. I hear the patter of rain on the roof. I start humming a song from long ago, "Rain on the roof — I love to hear the pitter patter of the rain on the roof."

Lettie enters with my coffee. "It's too wet outside."

"Where's Victoria?" I ask.

"She's in school. You were sleeping." She leaves.

I smile at the thought of the two Kirks in the rain. Should I get them an umbrella? I laugh and get up and take my cup to the desk. I must do some work on my book. I pick up a yellow pad and pencil and look out the window at the steady rain. My nude girl is drenched, rain pouring over her tiny breasts and long slim legs. The rain darkens her like a Nubian virgin.

I keep looking at her as I write: "My nude girl is standing in the rain, but she doesn't mind. She seems to be deep in thought. Where does she come from?"

I put my pencil down and look at what I have written. If my assistant, Grace, who has helped me with every word of this book, can decipher it, I will put it in.

I imagine that when the artist sculpted my nude girl, they fell in love and they got married. I write, "For many years he would sell his works of art, but never the girl I am looking at in the rain. He didn't want anyone else to see her nude. They got old together and he could no longer hold a chisel. He was forced to sell the nude girl and here she stands."

As I totter past ninety, I have learned something very important about love. I found that when I was young, I was incapable of deep love because so much of me was wound up with myself. Romance begins at eighty.

Seriously. The older you are, the more romantic you become. I think this is in part because you think less of yourself and more of your lover. In a long marriage, too often, romance is forgotten. But without romance, a marriage loses its vitality. To keep your marriage vibrant, dare to be romantic.

If you annoy your wife in a squabble and

she says something like, "I'm going to leave you," don't wait to find out if she means it. Quickly say, "If you ever leave me I'm going with you." That will bring back her smile.

Often, I pick the most beautiful rose in the garden for my wife and I put it in a small vase on her bedside table.

I write love poetry that would make Shakespeare wince, but — lucky me — Anne cherishes my poems for all occasions. Here is one:

Next to me lies a pillow
So soft, the color blue.
I crush the pillow to my chest
While I think of you
I peer at the clock above my head
How long will I be alone in bed?
Wait! I hear her —
I throw the pillow on the floor
I jump out of bed
And go for the door.
Soon you are in my arms
As I hold you tight.
Breath to breath, we are one
As we doze through the night.
Oh my darling, I love you
You make me feel so glad,
But the pillow lying on the floor
Is crushed and looks so sad.

What's wrong with being corny?

And while you are at it, learn to lie a little. When she gets dressed to go out, say, "Honey, you have never been more beautiful."

Also, most important, don't just give your wife a little peck on the cheek. Say, "Honey, I want a hug." And then press her to your body in a firm embrace.

If your wife works at an office, as mine does, from time to time call her and sing, "I just called to say I love you," and hang up.

Talk to her — or listen — while she is taking a bath. When she steps out of the tub, wrap her in a towel and help her dry off.

When I sit in the passenger seat beside the driver (fame and fortune has its benefits), I reach my arm over the seat toward Anne in the backseat. I wiggle my fingers. In time Anne notices and clasps my fingers for a few seconds. Nothing is said.

In the evening, fix your wife a drink. But make sure you know exactly how she likes it — not too much water.

When you go to bed and your wife's feet are cold, don't hesitate, let her rub them against your leg or back. The rewards will be fantastic.

When you are having breakfast in a hotel, don't forget to split apart the croissant and spread a little butter and honey on it. Don't eat it; offer it to her.

You're never too old to play games. Sometimes, on a weekend morning, I just loll in bed. The French call that *faire la grasse matinée.* The French always have a word or two on bed behavior. I know; I met my wife in Paris.

Not long after we were married in 1954, I learned that women love surprises. We were living in Palm Springs. It was Anne's birthday. I told her I couldn't be with her because I would be shooting a night scene for *Strangers When We Meet* in Los Angeles with Kim Novak.

She understood and invited a few of our friends to a Palm Springs restaurant for a birthday dinner without me.

I had lied. There was no night shooting. I finished my work by 5 p.m. and hired a truck to pick up a giant birthday cake that had been used in *Some Like It Hot.* The truck followed me to the restaurant.

At the appropriate time, they wheeled the cake to my wife's table. As everyone sang "Happy Birthday," I popped out of the cake.

Anne has done many wonderful things to help people. When she became a U.S.

citizen she wanted to do something to show her appreciation. After her two bouts with cancer she became very active, helping to raise millions of dollars for cancer research. She also founded the Anne Douglas Center for Homeless Women, which provides women with a comfortable place to live, classes to prepare them for better jobs, and help in curing drug or alcohol addictions. I'm proud of what she has accomplished.

We had an important collection of paintings that we had bought over the years: Picasso, Chagall, Miró, Vlaminck. Anne convinced me to sell them and put the money into our charitable foundation.

Anne is most proud of what she has done to help children. When she read in the *Los Angeles Times* that the L.A. school playgrounds were decrepit and dangerous, she decided to replace all of them with safe new equipment and rubberized flooring. I didn't think she could accomplish such a goal, but I misjudged my wife.

I accompany Anne at each playground inauguration. It's a treat to see the shining faces of our future Americans.

After Anne had renovated two hundred playgrounds we went to Washington, D.C., where I watched her receive the Jefferson Gold Medal for Extraordinary Services of a

Private Citizen.

"Anne, I'm so proud of you," I said. "What can I do to help?"

"Get a job!" she replied. "We need the money."

I'm still looking.

So far she has built more than 355 playgrounds for the children of Los Angeles.

I give to charity for selfish reasons. It makes me feel good.

During one's lifetime everyone should do something to help others. Then in the twilight of their years people can look back with satisfaction and say, "I did something."

Judaism insists that charity (*tzedakah*) be a motivating force in the life of every Jew. It's also important that charity be given in a way that is not degrading to the one accepting it. Maimonides says, "The reward of a good deed is the good deed, and the punishment for sin is sin."

Tomorrow ends our weekend in Montecito, and my wife, still in her dressing gown, is working at her computer. From my side of the bed I call out, "Honey, would you crawl into bed and cuddle with me? I'll give you a thousand dollars."

She throws a small pillow at my head — the pillow is a gift from the grandchildren and is embroidered with the saying "Grandmas Are Antique Little Girls."

"What do you think I am?" she asks.

"We know what you are, we're just talking price."

"That's an old joke," she says as a bigger pillow hits me, embroidered "Children Are a Great Comfort in Your Old Age. They Help You Reach It Sooner."

I chuckle. There is only silence but for the typing on her computer. I say, "I'll give you two thousand dollars."

Anne stops typing and approaches the bed, "How much?"

"Two thousand dollars."

I hear the swish of her dressing gown dropping off. She crawls into bed and begins to cuddle me.

I am so glad I'm rich. It's worth two thousand dollars. As we cuddle together, I make a feeble attempt at romance. "Honey, will you marry me again?"

She answers, "Why don't we wait until this weekend is over?"

I almost fall out of bed.

15
NEVER FORGET

When I was growing up, there were no black people in my neighborhood. There were none in the school I attended either. In college I don't remember seeing any blacks. But while studying in the library I came across a copy of an 1858 newspaper advertisement from Natchez, Mississippi:

SLAVES, SLAVES, SLAVES!!! HAVE JUST ARRIVED, FIELD-HANDS, COOKS, AND OTHERS.

Right under this ad was another:

MULES, MULES, MULES!!! JUST ARRIVED IN EXCELLENT CONDITION.

That shocked me. In school we didn't discuss slavery and I never thought much about it. I looked at that cruel advertisement and wondered, What would an African

American think about seeing this now?

The more I learned about African Americans, the more shocked I became. In my mind I saw a montage of signs: "the back of the bus" and "for colored only." I read about the lynching of black Americans in the South. All this happened after the Civil War and African Americans were supposed to be free.

Jews have much in common with blacks. We were both banished from our homelands, we both had to endure slavery, and we both had a history of exclusion.

We see the commonality between blacks and Jews in the speeches of Martin Luther King Jr. We hear it in African American spirituals: "Swing Low, Sweet Chariot"; "The Battle of Jericho"; and so many others. We hear it in the songs of Jewish composers, such as Harold Arlen's "Get Happy," with its lyric "C'mon get happy, we're goin' to the promised land" (the story of Exodus). Arlen spent much time in Harlem listening to artists like Duke Ellington, Louis Armstrong, and Fats Waller. Ethel Waters, who first sang his "Stormy Weather," called Arlen "the negroest white man I ever knew."

Arlen was hardly the only Jewish composer to write about blacks. Jerome Kern wrote about life on the Mississippi River with

Showboat, and George Gershwin spent a lot of time in South Carolina before he wrote *Porgy and Bess.*

When Johnny Mathis was very young, he auditioned to play the small part of a singer in a picture, *Lizzie,* for my production company. I chose the song "It's Not for Me to Say," which became a big hit — the song made more money than the movie did. Many years later he gave me a CD of him singing "Kol Nidre," the song that opens the High Holiday Yom Kippur — the Day of Atonement. I couldn't believe how beautifully he sang it, in perfect Hebrew. I'm trying to arrange for him to sing the song at the next Yom Kippur service at the Sinai Temple in Beverly Hills.

Every year I attend a Passover Seder, a dinner that commemorates the Jewish people's exodus from Egypt and the end of their slavery. Passover (Pesach) refers to the fact that God passed over the houses of the Jews when He slew the firstborn of Egypt. Each of the ritual foods is symbolic: There is *karpas,* usually parsley dipped in salt water, which symbolizes the lowly origins of the Jewish people. The salt water symbolizes the tears shed because of our slavery. *Maror* is most often raw horseradish, which stands for the bitterness of slavery. We dip it in a mixture of apples, nuts, cinnamon, and wine, which represents the mortar the Jews used in building while they were slaves. We eat matzo, unleavened bread, because the Jews left in such a hurry that they baked the dough in the desert sun.

The Seder is an elaborate dinner interspersed with songs and blessings. This complicated meal is celebrated each year to mark the slavery that ended more than three thousand years ago. It is a reminder of what happened and the closure to that period, which marks the beginning of the Jewish people. I would like to think that this dinner commemorates the end to all slavery.

The U.S. civil rights movement was the first step toward an honest confrontation with the subject of slavery. Hollywood has been able to depict slavery for an ever-larger audience. Movies and television shows such as *Roots, Glory, Beloved,* and *Amistad,* and the documentaries *Unchained Memories* and *Slavery and the Making of America* helped to make us face the tragedy. We have made enormous progress in our country, but much prejudice remains. In the entertainment world there is a great deal of assimilation, though bigotry still exists.

African Americans should celebrate with a

holiday like Passover as a reminder of what they endured. Of course we have Martin Luther King Jr. day, celebrating the civil rights movement, but that's not enough. They must never forget. Jews must never forget that we were once slaves under Pharaoh, thousands of years ago. And no one apologized.

President Bush recently made a trip to Africa, a fascinating continent now ravaged by AIDS. Africa needs our help. In Senegal, Mr. Bush stood on the shore of Gorée Island. From this spot, at least a million black Africans, shackled and chained, departed for a far-off country, America.

Standing beside the president was his then national security adviser, Condoleezza Rice, and Colin Powell, then secretary of state, listening to the president speak about this dark side of our history: "One of the largest forced migrations of history was also one of the greatest crimes in history."

What were Condoleezza Rice, a black American woman, and Colin Powell, a black American man, thinking when they heard these words? We never apologized. A whole race of people was treated as less than human and denied all the protection under the law that was extended to all other citizens. A closure to these injustices might be reached with a strong apology. How can we apologize for these awful crimes of inhumanity that we inflicted?

The slaves came from Africa. Our apology would best be expressed by trying to solve the problems that exist in Africa now — genocide, poverty, rape, starvation, and corruption. The apology should not just be a token sum of money sent to Africa, which might be stolen by government officials. The apology should be a gigantic movement of money, food, personnel, and the military. It should be comparable to the Marshall Plan at the end of World War II. At that time, the world looked approvingly upon our country because we showed concern for others.

We have lost much of that approval in recent times. Instead of trying to spread democracy with a gun, let it be by example. Think of how it would benefit the world if we took the trillions of dollars we spend on military strength and instead used the money to help other people. Let our motto not be "Bring it on!" but rather "Caring is sharing."

America is the strongest country in the world, the only superpower. We believe that all people are created equal, so let our actions prove it. Let's show the world a concrete example of what democracy means — caring for others, not conquering them.

16
BE THE PERSON YOUR DOGS THINK YOU ARE

I'm in my den playing spider solitaire on my computer. Danny and Foxy are watching me. I lose again. I turn off the computer. With my left hand I scratch Danny's back. His tail wags approvingly. With my right hand I do the same to Foxy, as his tail wags in unison with Danny's. They adore me. They want only to be near me, with the hope that I'll scratch their backs. They think I can do no wrong.

I get up and flop onto the bed. I slap the cover and Danny quickly jumps up beside me. Foxy hops onto the foot of the bed. This is their routine. They fall asleep immediately.

I continue to scratch Danny's back. He reminds me so much of a dog, Banshee, I had years ago during the McCarthy period, many years before Danny arrived on the scene.

Banshee was a beautiful yellow Labrador

and his remains lie under a rock in my rose garden. Banshee once helped me to stand up for freedom of speech. I was reminded of this one night while watching George Clooney's movie *Good Night, and Good Luck,* which re-created newscaster Edward R. Murrow's famous broadcast against Senator Joseph McCarthy. George Clooney did a wonderful job — acting, writing, and directing.

Anne and I knew Edward R. Murrow from an interview we did with him on his show *Person to Person.* Luckily, no one made a movie about our broadcast.

McCarthy began seeing communists in Congress, the military, and the White House. He then concentrated on Hollywood, especially on writers.

In 1947 the House Un-American Activities Committee started to interrogate people who'd been accused of holding left-wing views, most of them writers. A few people buckled under the pressure of the committee, but most refused to answer the committee's demands to disclose the names of others. A second round of investigations into communism in Hollywood questioned Larry Parks, who had a big hit playing Al Jolson in *The Jazz Singer.* I knew him; he was a talented, gentle guy. He died soon after he was questioned by the committee.

Everyone who was called before the committee went on the blacklist if they didn't deny they were communists and if they refused to name others. More than 320 people were deemed uncooperative and were blacklisted as the frightened heads of the Hollywood studios readily fell in step with the hysteria. They wouldn't hire anyone who was even *suspected* of being a communist. Imagine — these people were denied an opportunity to make a living whether they were in fact communists or not. Many writers fled to foreign countries in search of work; others stayed here and continued to write scripts, surreptitiously, under assumed names. The studios looked the other way but insisted that the writer's real name never be revealed and that the writer never appear at the studio. Such hypocrisy!

Dalton Trumbo was one of the Hollywood Ten who received a one-year jail sentence. At the time, my production company, the Bryna Company, was producing *Spartacus* with backing from Universal Pictures. The book had been written by Howard Fast, who was also under scrutiny by McCarthy's committee. We had an all-star cast for this epic: Laurence Olivier, Peter Ustinov,

Charles Laughton, Jean Simmons, and Tony Curtis. I played the part of Spartacus, a slave in Roman times who led a revolt against the emperor. I'm ashamed to admit that I joined the hypocrites by employing Dalton Trumbo secretly to write the script under the pseudonym of Sam Jackson.

Since he was not allowed to come to the studio, we would meet like thieves in the night at his house. He usually received us while soaking in the bathtub, with a parrot — a gift from me — perched on his shoulder. He wrote a wonderful script and we were in the middle of making a fantastic picture.

Our director, Anthony Mann, was a very nice guy whom the studio insisted on using. I was against it. A few weeks into the picture, the studio said, "Kirk, you were right. Fire Anthony Mann." That was very difficult for me but I did it. I felt that I owed him something, though, and a few years later I acted in a picture under his direction, *The Heroes of Telemark*.

It was the end of the week. Here was one of the biggest-budget pictures in Hollywood history shooting without a director. Then I heard that Marlon Brando was starring in *One-Eyed Jacks,* which was being directed by Stanley Kubrick. Marlon fired Stanley and took over the direction himself. (He did a good job, too.) In a minute I was on the phone with Stanley and during that weekend arranged for him to become the new director of *Spartacus*.

On Monday morning the cast, in makeup and costumes, gathered in the gladiator stadium looking down into the arena. They were all gossiping about who was going to be the new director. I walked into the arena with Stanley and called up to them, "This is your new director — Stanley Kubrick!" There was silence as they looked down in bewilderment at this young director. Stanley was about twenty-six years old, but he looked sixteen. Stanley looked up at them — Laurence Olivier, Charles Laughton, Peter Ustinov, Jean Simmons, Tony Curtis — with complete confidence. We made a terrific picture.

Then the question came up as to what name we should use on the screen for the screenwriter. I felt awkward using "Sam Jackson." It was so hypocritical. Our country was in danger of losing one of our freedoms. Talented people were not allowed to use their names because McCarthy had spread such a veil of suspicion over them. What would happen next? It made me feel unclean.

I talked with my producer, Eddie Lewis, and Stanley. Stanley suggested, "Put my name on the screen as the writer."

I was shocked. "Stanley," I asked, "wouldn't you feel funny taking credit for a script you had nothing to do with?"

He said, "Not at all."

"Stanley, we started filming the script before you came on the picture."

"I'm only trying to help you out," he answered.

I looked at Eddie and saw disgust in his face.

That night, in bed, I couldn't get it off my mind. I had to make a decision. I slapped the bed and Banshee jumped up and lay down next to me. I stroked his back — I could almost hear him purr. "Banshee," I asked, "how would you like to be called Rover? Here, Rover!"

Banshee looked at me quizzically.

I smiled and went to sleep. I had made my decision.

At the studio the next morning I told Eddie and Stanley, "I've decided to use Dalton Trumbo's name on the screen."

Eddie smiled at me with approval. He was always against the blacklist.

Stanley looked at me, said, "You must be crazy," and left the room.

Eddie and I were stunned, but I was determined to put "Written by Dalton Trumbo" on the screen for the first time in ten years.

The next day I invited Dalton to the studio. I left a pass for him at the gate. He looked at Eddie and me and said with a wry smile, "This is the first time I have been in a studio in ten years. Thanks for giving me back my name."

It was the most important decision that I made in my career. We never held a press conference but word got out. People said I had ruined my career, that I would never work again. Otto Preminger called from New York, quite upset. He was directing *Exodus,* which Dalton Trumbo had also written under an assumed name. In his German accent he said, "Vat are you doing? Are you crazy? Don't do dat!"

I answered, "Otto, it's done."

He hung up the phone. Soon he held a press conference to announce that he would give credit to Dalton Trumbo as the writer of *Exodus.* Otto was a smart producer. He didn't want to be caught using a nom de plume for Dalton Trumbo when I was using Trumbo's real name.

Despite all that he had gone through, Dalton kept his sense of humor. He gave me a copy of his book *Johnny Got His Gun.* Everywhere that it said "Dalton Trumbo" he had crossed the name out and written "Sam Jackson." On the flyleaf he wrote,

Here, for what it is, and for what I hope I still am, is the only existing copy of this book that's signed with the name to which I was born, and the other name you've enabled me to acquire under circumstances that blessedly permit me to respect and to *cherish* both the new name and the new friend who made it possible.

He signed it with both signatures — Dalton Trumbo and his pseudonym, Sam Jackson.

When *Spartacus* was released there were lots of reactions, both positive and negative: "Kirk, you're a hero," "Kirk, you're a shmuck!" "What's the matter, you don't want to work in this town anymore?" Hedda Hopper, an important columnist at the time, lambasted me: ". . . from a book written by a Commie and the screen script written by a Commie, so don't go to see it."

A few people wrote threatening letters, but the sky didn't fall in. The blacklist was broken. And the movie was a success.

I can't think of anything in my life that

made me more proud. Sometimes you just have to be the person your dog thinks you are.

Our freedoms — freedom of speech, freedom of worship, freedom to believe what we want to believe — are very fragile and they must constantly be protected. Yes, even now.

17
CEMETERIES

A visit to a cemetery now and again is good for the soul. It reminds us that we are mortal and have no time to waste.

I make visits to the grave of my mother in Albany and to the grave of my father outside Amsterdam, New York. I never heard my mother say an unkind word about my father, but she insisted that she wanted to be buried separately. I tried to talk her out of it without success — it just seemed right to me that in death they should be together — but my mother prevailed.

This made me realize how much my mother must have suffered because of my father. My mother always called my father by his name, Herschel. Yet I never heard my father call my mother by her name, Bryna. He would say, "Hey," or, "Tell the Mrs.," but never "Bryna." That's why I call my company Bryna.

Ma is buried in an overcrowded cemetery

in Albany with a garden of huge tombstones. On the other hand, my father is buried in a quiet, serene cemetery in Amsterdam. It has a brook that runs along the edge and many trees for shade, and it's very peaceful.

We had a house in Palm Springs for forty years. Frank Sinatra was often a guest there and we frequently went to his house. Now he lies in a cemetery in Palm Springs with acres and acres of verdant grass. The graves are indicated by flat metal markers. Engraved is the name and the dates of birth and death.

I knew Frank for many, many years. I gave his eulogy in a Los Angeles chapel with Cardinal John J. Mahoney sitting not far from me. In the eulogy I told his wife, "Barbara, when Frank meets Dean Martin and Sammy Davis up there, heaven will never be the same." Cardinal Mahoney laughed the loudest.

The last time I was in Palm Springs I went to visit Frank's grave. I walked across the closely cropped lawn. First, I came upon the plaque marking where his father, Martin, was buried. Then the one for his mother, Dolly; she had been flying to meet Frank in Las Vegas, and the plane crashed in the mountains that surround Palm Springs.

Nearby was a marker for Frank's uncle. I hadn't known him. Next was Frank's grave, with the same-size plaque.

THE BEST IS YET TO COME
Francis Albert
SINATRA
1915–1998

It was difficult to read because his marker was heaped with flowers and covered with pennies. Pennies from heaven?

On his birthday, December 12 (three days after mine), people come to his grave from all over the world to celebrate with an orchestra. The group becomes rowdy. This quiet afternoon I stood at the grave of my friend. "Frank, remember how we celebrated your eightieth birthday?" I asked. "We planned to have dinner at L'Orangerie, but the paparazzi were ahead of us. We were warned that a horde of photographers was waiting at the restaurant. Many, in cars, collected at your front gate. Jolene and George Schlatter, close friends of ours, solved the problem. They live nearby and we decided to have the dinner at their house. The plan worked out perfectly. A limo drove up your driveway. We put Vi, your favorite maid, and a butler in the backseat. They drove off and the paparazzi gave chase. The rest of us met you at the Schlatters' and had a wonderful birthday party. Remember, Frank?"

It was a very quiet afternoon and I enjoyed talking to Frank. "Francis, I will tell you one story we never talked about. You were staying with your new wife, Ava Gardner, in the Hampshire House in New York. I was staying there, too, shooting a picture, *The Brotherhood.* One night as I slept I heard a knock at the door. I woke up, looked at my clock. Two o'clock! Who could that be? I wondered. I went to the door, opened it, and there was Ava Gardner crying. I led her into the room, sat her down, and tried to console her. The story she told startled me. 'Frank and I had an argument. He has a gun. He threatened to commit suicide. I don't know what to do.' I gave her a drink of water to calm her down. 'Ava, married people have arguments. I know. Frank loves you. You must go back and try to act like nothing happened.'

"You know, Frank, we never mentioned that incident. But you finally got it right when you married Barbara. Over twenty years with her must have convinced you that she was one hell of a girl." I started counting the pennies on Frank's grave. I gave up at about forty and I left.

My son Eric is buried in a unique cemetery. The burial grounds are not in some far-off place but smack in the center of Westwood, next to Beverly Hills, surrounded by high-rise apartments. The dead amid so much thriving life. In the middle of all that activity it is peaceful. I wonder if the people looking down from their dwellings reflect on the fact that this will be their final destination. It's only a five- or ten-minute drive from my home.

Whenever my wife and I go there, we sit on the bench and think of our son and talk to him. Some thoughts are happy, some are sad, but these visits bring us closer to Eric and help us to endure the tragedy.

Many people I knew are in this cemetery. Al Toffel was a friend of mine; he married Steve McQueen's former wife, Neile. One weekend, they went to Las Vegas to see some shows and have a good time. While getting dressed to go out, he fell to the floor, sank into a coma, and never recovered. He died from a massive heart attack. He was only sixty-nine.

Al was a happy guy. He would do anything for a laugh. Once he gave me a clown wig, a red rubber nose, and big clown shoes painted red and white. He liked to see me dress up in his gift and sing, "Be a clown, be a clown." We laughed together.

He objected to my black cane, which helped me with my bad knees. "It's too sad," he said. "Too formal for a guy like you." His last gift to me was a "happy cane," carved in patterns painted yellow, green, and red. I was leaning on my happy cane when his coffin was carried to the burial site. I will miss him.

Close by his grave is a plaque that reads: "Natalie Wood Wagner." What a beautiful girl! What a tragic death!

On a quiet day I like to walk around this place where so many of my colleagues were buried. Walter Matthau and Jack Lemmon are here, close even in death. The last time I saw Jack, we were playing poker at Barbara Sinatra's house.

Rodney Dangerfield was recently buried here. "No respect!" he would cry out from the stage, but he earned everyone's respect for his gigantic talent.

Another marker says "Louis Jourdan," Quique and Louis's son. He committed suicide in his twenties — a handsome boy, and troubled. I remember him telling me how much he wanted a car. I said I was sure that if he could show his parents that he was responsible, they would give him one. I got him a job in a food market. I talked to his guitar instructor and convinced Louis to play his guitar again. I thought he was improving — and now here he lies.

Whenever I pass by Mel Tormé's slab, I can hear that velvet voice singing "Night and Day." Near him is Sammy Cahn — what a character, what a great lyricist! He built a house opposite mine and asked to stay in my guesthouse for a weekend to oversee its construction. I agreed. He stayed there for three months. When Anne and I left for Europe, he moved into our big house. Then we came back and were afraid he wouldn't move out, but he did. He was frugal with his money but very generous with his talent and very kind. Sammy wrote the song that Burt Lancaster and I sang at the Oscars, "It's Great Not to Be Nominated." The hit songs he wrote are too numerous to mention, but I will never forget "My Love," "All the Way," and a song that he wrote for Sinatra, "My Kind of Town."

In this cemetery there is a structure composed of vaults, one placed upon the other, with the names of the deceased on small plaques. It's always easy to recognize the vault containing Marilyn Monroe. Joe DiMaggio, the famous baseball player and one of Marilyn's ex-husbands, arranged for fresh flowers to be placed in the metal urn attached to her vault every day. Every time I walk by, visitors are looking at the name Marilyn Monroe. Poor Marilyn, she never found the happiness that her fame denied her.

I remember the first time I met Marilyn, at the home of producer Sam Spiegel. The only woman in the room, she sat quietly in a chair watching Sam play gin rummy with friends and hoping that he'd get her a job in movies. I felt sorry for her. I tried to talk with her, but it wasn't much of a conversation.

On the screen Marilyn came to life. She was a different person.

My God, cemeteries, suicides, burials! But, of course, life also has some happy times.

18
A Whale of a Tale

Last year while Anne was preparing my eighty-ninth birthday party, I went into the garden and was drawn like a magnet to look at my dual busts. Young Kirk was still a smiling twenty-seven and old Kirk a dignified eighty-six.

Michael, who lives in Bermuda, almost didn't make it to my birthday. When he realized I was only eighty-nine, he was disappointed.

"Eighty-nine is nothing," he said, "but ninety!"

He came anyway and brought his son Cameron. That made it five boys: Michael, Joel, Peter, Cameron, and me.

I nervously waited for them to pick me up. I had to laugh at myself. I felt like a giddy girl waiting to be picked up for the prom.

They entered the house together — so tall, handsome, and filled with love. They took me to my favorite L.A. restaurant, L'Orangerie, and when our glasses were filled we made the first toast to Eric. Eric had loved his brothers. If he was watching us from heaven, it had to be with a smile.

All my sons have a good sense of humor. The second toast was proposed by Joel — "A toast to Kirk Douglas Way!" This was a street recently named after me in Palm Springs.

Please don't be impressed by the honors I have received. I'm not. If you live long enough you get them all.

Michael called out, "Are you writing a new book, Dad?

"Yes, I'm trying."

Joel asked, "What's that, your ninth book?"

Before I could answer, Peter interrupted, "Please, Dad, don't make it too Jewish." We all laughed and had another drink. We were unaware of the other patrons until the birthday cake arrived and the whole restaurant — customers, waiters, and bartenders — joined my family in singing "Happy Birthday."

Our table was the only one in the bar, not far from the piano player. Suddenly, on cue, she started playing "A Whale of a Tale," a song I sang years ago in the movie *20,000*

Leagues Under the Sea. The recording of me singing the song was very popular at the time.

All of my kids know the song and they taught it to their kids. We began to sing in unison:

Got a whale of a tale to tell ya, lads,
A whale of a tale or two
'Bout the flapping fish and the girls I've
    loved
On nights like this with the moon above
A whale of a tale and it's all true
I swear by my tattoo

There was Mermaid Minnie, met her down
    in Madagascar
She would kiss me, any time that I would
    ask her
Then one evening her flame of love blew
    out
Blow me down and pick me up
She swapped me for a trout

Got a whale of a tale . . .

By then Joel, who has the best voice, was singing alone — he was the only one who could remember the rest of the lyrics.

I looked at Cameron, tall, handsome, full

of charm, and very talented. In his youth, he had always gotten into trouble.

When he was twenty, I thought I should have a serious talk with him.

"Cameron, you have to do something with your life. Get a job."

"I have a job, Pappy."

That surprised me. "What do you do?"

"I'm a DJ," he answered.

I had no idea what that was. "Well, how much money can you make doing that?"

"About five thousand dollars."

"Five thousand dollars a year?"

"A week!"

I was stunned. I tell you, I can't keep up with the younger generation, but I worry about them.

I looked at my watch; it was getting late. The next morning Anne and I had to attend a playground inauguration. This would be our 355th playground. We've gone to all of the inaugurations and we've seen a lot of young citizens. I love to watch the youngest of them, all dressed up, their faces shining, playing on their new playground. This is a happy world for them, but they will grow up.

They can't see their future now.

What will their future be? Dirty air . . .

contaminated water . . . global warming . . . deficits . . . corruption . . . cronyism . . . invasion of privacy . . . religious squabbles . . . poor education . . . suicide bombers . . . nuclear destruction? Will they think we failed them? Will they curse us?

I won't be there. I'll be lying on a grassy riverbank under the shade of a eucalyptus tree. One hand will be in the cool water as I listen to the muted cacophony of the world.

Let's face it — I'll be dead.

19
I LOVE DOGS

As I think you know by now, I love dogs. All my life we have had a dog or two or three. Years ago, we had a small poodle, Teddy. Teddy loved Anne. While we ate dinner, he would sit in a chair in the corner. When dessert was served, he would jump up on Anne's lap. How did he know it was time for dessert? I never found out.

Teddy was quite a dog. At night, he slept under the blankets at Anne's feet. I was surprised he never suffocated. One day I came home after a week of shooting on location. That night I crawled into bed with my wife. When I reached over to embrace her, Teddy began to growl. I left the bed, waited for a moment, and quietly went in again. The growl was louder. This annoyed me, but my wife was laughing. Teddy ruined my night.

Once we had a black Labrador named Shaft, who was actually more my son Peter's dog. When I made a movie in Yugoslavia I took Peter and Eric along, and Peter insisted on Shaft coming with us. The movie, *Scalawag,* had a scene in which a vicious dog attacks one of the men. We found a dog in the village that the owner said would do the job. Yes, he could do the job, but this was a movie. The dog attacked Danny DeVito, who was playing in his first role — just like the dog, come to think of it. We had to pull the dog off him.

Peter said that Shaft could do it. I was uncertain because Shaft was such an affectionate dog, but Peter arranged for the actor to have some food hidden in his pocket, and he trained Shaft to go after the food. As the cameras rolled, Shaft raced in and jumped all over the man, looking for the food. He barked joyously. We took the audio portions with his barks out of the scene and added the growls and barks of the local dog that had been fired. It worked perfectly.

Recently, I put Danny and Foxy into a scene in *Illusion,* lying with me in bed. They were okay, but they were no Shaft. Shaft was the only movie-star dog in our family.

I close my eyes and think of all our dogs. One weekend Michael brought this big German shepherd that had the same name as my late Laborador, Banshee, home from college.

My wife said, "Please keep him away from my little Teddy."

"Oh, Banshee is very gentle," replied Michael. Famous last words.

We were in Anne's room and Teddy was on the bed snarling at Banshee, who was entering the room with Michael.

"He's very gentle," Michael assured us again as Banshee approached the bed.

Teddy came toward Banshee yapping loudly, protecting his territory. When Teddy got closer, Banshee opened his mouth and almost seemed to swallow him. Michael quickly pulled his dog back and Teddy flopped on the bed, stiff as though in rigor mortis.

My wife wailed, "He's dead! He's dead!"

"He can't be," Michael assured us. But Teddy didn't move.

"Let's get him to a vet," I said. I picked up Teddy, stiff, and we hurried to drive to the vet. Needless to say, the German shepherd was not with us. Michael was quiet and feeling very guilty.

At the vet, we sat silently waiting for the doctor. Teddy was still not moving. My wife was shooting daggers at Michael.

Suddenly, Teddy twitched his nose, jumped off my lap, ran over to the corner, and urinated for a long time. After that, he was fine.

Each death of a dog you love is like a death of a family member. Teddy died at five. My Banshee lived to be twelve. I thought of Danny, nine, and Foxy, five. Will I still be alive to mourn them when they die? Why do dogs die at an early age? If there is an afterlife, will there be dogs? I would hate to live without a dog in any life. They have been such a help to me.

I don't know who wrote the story about the Rainbow Bridge, which supposedly lies next to heaven. According to this story, when your pet dies, that's where it goes — the Rainbow Bridge. He or she meets other pets and they run and play together on the meadows and hills, and there is enough food, water, and sunshine.

The story goes: "All the animals who have been ill and old are restored to health and the vigor of youth. Those who were abused, hurt or maimed are made whole and strong again, just as we would want to remember them in our dreams of days and times gone by."

When Danny and Foxy go to the Rainbow

Bridge they'll be young and healthy and Foxy will have perfect vision. They'll be happy except for one thing: they will miss someone who loved them — someone who took care of them. Then one day Danny will suddenly stop and look off into the distance. Foxy will, too. With a yelp, Danny will begin to run, Foxy following. They will have spotted me, and Danny and Foxy will climb all over me in a joyous reunion.

20
TRYING OUR BEST

Walter Savage Landor, a poet, seventy-six years old, decided to write his epitaph:

I fought with none for none was worth my
   strife.
Nature I loved, and next to Nature, Art.
I warmed both hands 'gainst the fire of life,
It stinks and I am ready to depart.

He lived to be eighty-eight — twelve years after he wrote his epitaph. Should I think about writing my own epitaph? I don't have to think about it. I know what it will be:
"I tried, dammit, I tried!"

That's what the character Randle P. Mc-Murphy cries out in Ken Kesey's novel *One Flew Over the Cuckoo's Nest.* That's also the advice I've given to all my sons. Whatever you do, try your best. Then, even if you fail, you know that you couldn't have done more.

I loved *One Flew Over the Cuckoo's Nest,* so I bought the dramatic rights to it. I paid Dale Wasserman to write a play based on it and I went off to New York to fulfill my lifelong ambition of being a Broadway star. The year was 1963 and, after the success of *Spartacus,* I was at the top of my movie career. My agents were against my leaving such a lucrative niche in Hollywood, but I didn't listen to them. I took no salary and played the part of McMurphy for six months. The critics killed it.

While trying out the play in Boston, where it received rave reviews, I got a note from Dr. Timothy Leary at Harvard University. He invited me to join "a mind-expansion group." That sounded exciting and I was eager to do it, but I didn't have the time. Later I found out that Ken Kesey was part of a group that contributed to the wide use of LSD and other hallucinogenic drugs in the sixties.

I invited Ken to New York to see the play. He had written the book, so I thought he should see the play. He disagreed with most of the critics — he liked it.

After six months, though, I gave up trying to succeed on the stage. I had tried my best, and I had failed. I came back to Hollywood and for ten years attempted to make a movie out of *One Flew Over the Cuckoo's Nest*. Again, I tried my best and failed.

My son Michael was just finishing his fourth year in the TV series *The Streets of San Francisco* with my friend Karl Malden. Michael came to me one day and asked, "Dad, why don't you let me try to do something with Ken Kesey's book?"

"Go ahead. I tried for ten years." I had no confidence that he would succeed after all of my years of effort.

Within a year he put the movie together and was ready to shoot. I was dumbfounded.

"Who is your director?" I asked.

"You wouldn't know him, Dad."

"What's his name?"

"Milos Forman."

I couldn't believe it. Several years earlier, when I was on a tour of Europe for the United States Information Agency, I had met Forman in Prague. I had seen two of his films and was very impressed. I was so impressed that I told him I would send him a book that I loved. You guessed it: *One Flew Over the Cuckoo's Nest.* I sent it, but he never received it. Communist countries at that time were leery of books.

Yet even with my own son producing the movie, I couldn't get a break. I tried to get the part I had played on Broadway.

Michael came back with, "I'm sorry, Dad. I tried."

"What do you mean you tried? You're the producer."

"He's the director. He thinks you're too old."

"Too old!"

I was devastated that Forman didn't want me to play the part of McMurphy. Too old. (I had been much younger in Prague.) They gave it to a talented newcomer, Jack Nicholson, who won an Oscar for his performance. He deserved it. Michael received his first Oscar, as a producer. In fact, the movie received Oscars in all the five top categories.

My *naches* — gratification, in Yiddish — from Michael's success surpassed my disappointment in having failed. Besides, he tried.

So remember — if you try and fail, something good can come from it. You might inspire someone else.

21
SOME OF MY BEST FRIENDS ARE ACTORS

Charles Jehlinger was the head of the American Academy of Dramatic Arts when I was a student there many years ago. We called him Mr. Jehlinger to his face and "Jelly" behind his back. He was short, about five feet, with blazing eyes behind thick spectacles. Over the years, lots of students came before him acting in plays on a small stage in the basement of Carnegie Hall. They included Spencer Tracy, Jennifer Jones, Lauren Bacall, Robert Redford, Grace Kelly, and many others.

Jelly would stand at the back of the theater and yell at us, "Any fool can learn lines and cues. Acting takes the finest use of the intellect!"

I was about twenty-one years old then. Over the next seven decades, I've discovered that he was correct.

In my most poignant memory of the academy — I've told this story before —

the student actors were sitting in a semi-circle before the instructor. The task was to play an owl. Each student got up and tried to be an owl. I thought they were awful and I couldn't wait to get my chance.

Sitting beside me was my friend Paul. He got up, formed his body into the shape of an owl, and hooted, "I'm an oold ooowl."

The instructor raised his hand to silence the class. He said, "Hooow ooold are you, owl?"

Paul ruffled his feathers and said, "I am verry ooold."

The instructor turned to the class and mouthed, "This is genius."

He never called on me. I was mad the entire day.

Many people think that actors are airheads and that once they finish spouting lines written by someone else, they have nothing original to say. I've found that all good actors are intelligent and multifaceted. I'm amazed at all the different talents displayed by entertainers.

Frank Sinatra was a fine artist. I liked his earlier paintings of real life. In his later years, his painting style became impressionistic, though, and I didn't care for it. Tony Curtis's paintings are displayed in many museums and the prices keep rising. Years ago, he gave me a painting of a big bowl of roses. I still have it. Tony Bennett is a better artist. When he first gave me a brochure of his paintings I was amazed. Viacom chairman Sumner Redstone has many of Tony's paintings hanging on the walls in his house. The price for one of his paintings continues to climb.

Steve Martin surprised me with his talent for writing plays.

Anthony Quinn was a good friend of mine. When I drive downtown to the Anne Douglas Center for Homeless Women I pass an old six-story building with a painting of Tony Quinn doing his dance in *Zorba the Greek*. What a performance! We did two pictures together — *The Last Train from Gun Hill* and *Lust for Life,* which earned him a Best Supporting Actor Oscar. Tony was a wonderful sculptor as well as a painter. His work is very powerful and he expressed his talent in many media. Out of friendship, he made me a set of cufflinks which I treasure highly.

Actors are also citizens, so they participate in politics as well. The media sometimes paint us as falling off the side of the left, but there are Democratic actors and Republican actors. In politics, the Republican actors have had more success. Ronald Reagan became president of the United States for two terms. George Murphy became a senator. Sonny Bono, the former husband of Cher, became a Republican congressman. Arnold Schwarzenegger married into the Democratic Kennedy clan but became a Republican governor.

In our country, there's so much stress on right and left. Religion, politics, patriotism, should all be unifying forces for the whole world but so often they are not.

In 1963 my wife and I were in Brazil for Carnaval. At the ball I wore my *Spartacus* outfit. Then I received a request from the White House asking me to stop over in Bogota, Colombia, to represent America in the film festival being held there. The warm reception I received in Brazil and Colombia gave me an idea: why not use movie stars as ambassadors of goodwill? All countries recognize us from the parts we play on the screen, but we are known as Americans first and are never considered Democrats, Republicans, conservatives, or liberals.

With my wife's help, I arranged an itinerary of countries that I would visit, giving talks to university students. I decided to pay all of my own expenses to avoid adverse criticism. The United States Information Agency (USIA) would be my host. My first visit was to Yugoslavia, where I bought the nude sculpture that now stands in my garden. I arrived in Belgrade and the USIA arranged for me to spend an evening at a bureaucrat's house, meeting with five students who were interested in making pictures. I told the USIA officer that I wanted to talk to a lot of students, not just those interested in movie making. He told me that was not possible in a communist country. He was wrong.

With a little effort I finally got the number of the university public relations office. I called, and someone answered in a language I didn't understand.

I said, "I'm Kirk Douglas."

He answered in broken English, "Don't make joke."

I finally convinced him I was who I said I was, which seemed to please him very much.

The next evening I spoke to several thousand students. Of course it was through an interpreter, but the students reacted like raucous American students. I told them about my background and about my illiterate parents from Russia, about poverty and my early school years. One anecdote from my childhood got a roar of laughter: I told them that when my first grade teacher explained to us how to brush our teeth, I asked, "Why do you have to brush the back of your teeth? Nobody sees it." Another laugh came when I said we didn't have money for toothpaste so we used salt. We really did. It's not bad; try it sometime.

The theme of my talk was that in America you have a chance. I told them about the opportunities I had been given to attend college and choose my profession. They were very receptive. I used a similar talk in most of the countries I visited.

The officials of other countries welcomed movie stars. They were all movie buffs! I visited Afghanistan, Austria, Bulgaria, China, Colombia, Egypt, Germany, Hong Kong, Hungary, India, Israel, Japan, Jordan, Pakistan, the Philippines, Romania, Russia, Thailand, Turkey, and, of course, Yugoslavia. Everywhere I talked to students, telling them my story.

I'm not alone. Many actors have used their position to help other countries, but it takes intelligence and sensitivity to feel the pain of others. Cameron Diaz, accompanied by Justin Timberlake and Drew Barrymore, visited impoverished areas in many countries around the world that need assistance.

Angelina Jolie is a UN goodwill ambassador. Brad Pitt has done his share, too. Brad and Angelina have spent a lot of time in Africa. She adopted an African baby and also gave birth to her own child in Africa. Angelina has given $3 million to help the children of Africa. Vanessa Redgrave, an extremely intelligent actress who has always been interested in world affairs, launched the Humanitarian Assistance Program at Fordham University. I also cannot forget the good work that Audrey Hepburn did as a UN goodwill ambassador. And Gary Sinise founded an operation that sends Iraqi children school supplies.

My son Michael received the Messenger of Peace award from the United Nations for his work in making a documentary in Sierra Leone in Africa. Rebels from Liberia were kidnapping young kids and taking them to their jungle hideout. There they filled them with dope and brainwashed them into becoming killers. One little boy of about twelve or fourteen had escaped and was trying to find his mother. Michael tried to communicate with this numb boy who never smiled. Michael placed his arm around the boy and sang a little song:

I love you a bushel and a peck,

A bushel and a peck and a hug around
the neck.

It made me cry, but it finally made the boy smile. Michael learned that the boy had no idea how many people he had killed, how many limbs he had chopped off. Finally, he was returned to his mother. Still, the rebels continue to infiltrate Sierra Leone and capture young boys and rape young girls.

Michael's wife, Catherine Zeta-Jones, also helps. She is an ambassador for the National Society for the Prevention of Cruelty to Children. Paul Newman contributes millions of dollars to charity through his company, which makes the best salad dressing you can find. The rock star Bono has traveled in many parts of the world, especially Africa, spreading goodwill. He has been warmly received by Nelson Mandela, Secretary of State Condoleezza Rice, and Pope John Paul II. All of Bono's efforts campaigning against poverty have earned him a nomination for a Nobel Peace Prize.

Some of my best friends are actors.

22
Can We Talk?

I'm walking around the pool again. It's a hot summer afternoon. Danny and Foxy don't follow me; they're too smart. They just watch me from a shady spot. What do they think of their master going out in the broiling sun?

I'm thinking about an article I read in the morning paper. During the wars in Afghanistan and Iraq, the military seems to be having a lot of problems recruiting people who speak Arabic to serve. I stop at the dual bust. The sun reflects off the steel. The busts don't seem to mind the hot sun and young Kirk is still smiling. He seems so smug, so sure of himself. He was a worker, though. Whenever we shot a picture in a foreign land he studied that language.

"*Parles-tu Français?*" I say to young Kirk, using the familiar form. "You were never intimidated by another language." He's *still* smiling. Once he learned a few expressions he thought he knew the language. He insisted on doing the French version of *Act of Love.* When they told him he didn't speak French, young Kirk said he would learn, and he did. He practiced his French lines on his girlfriend.

"Remember?" I asked him.

One scene went like this: *"Est-que vous êtes libre ce dimanche? J'ai pensé qu'on peut faire une promenade à la campagne — si vous êtes libre, c'est-à-dire."* (Are you free Sunday? I thought that we might take a walk in the country — if you are free, that is.) The French girls were so impressed with my French they always walked with me in the park.

We Americans are often too unworldly, and insist that everyone speak English. I learned that when I traveled for the USIA. Very often the Americans stationed in other countries assumed that everybody spoke English and they made no attempt to learn the language of the country. As a result, they were poorly informed about what was going on.

I sent a report about my trips to the USIA in Washington. I emphasized that not enough Americans spoke the language of each country. We had to depend on a citizen of that country for translation. Were they translating accurately? Not all the time. I don't even know if my report was ever read.

Visiting all of those foreign countries, even for a short time, was a wonderful experience for me. The crowning achievement was when President Jimmy Carter awarded me the Medal of Freedom, the highest civilian award that a U.S. citizen can receive. A few movie stars have received it, and I'm very proud to be one of them.

Although I paid all my own expenses, the U.S. Treasury tried to reimburse me for one of the trips. I sent the check back. They sent it back to me. I didn't want it. They wouldn't take it. I went through so many bureaucrats, I was at the point of keeping the check when I finally succeeded in returning the money to the taxpayers. After all, it's your money.

Maybe the younger generation will solve our country's language problems. One day Anne and I were having lunch with Dennis Miller and his beautiful wife, Carolyn. Dennis told us that his son Holden, fourteen years old, was going away to school. Holden said that he planned to study Chinese. "Chinese?!" Dennis replied. "Why not Spanish? That's a language you can use more often."

"Dad," Holden said patiently, "by the time

I grow up China will be a superpower. I want to be one American who can speak to them in their own language."

I was amazed! Are there more of our children who think like that? I hope so, because most Americans don't learn other languages.

To learn to speak another language takes courage. Don't be afraid of making a mistake — plunge in! I have found that in most countries people are pleased when you try to speak their language; they will help you.

In Italy, if you just say, "Ciao," they smile and reply, *"Lei parla italiano!"* (You speak Italian!)

France is different. I love the French, but I find they are not very helpful if you try to learn their language. In Paris, I spoke French to my driver. He always responded in English. I finally told him, "I want to learn to speak French. Why do you answer me in English?"

Haughtily, he said, "I want to learn English."

I fired him.

It will be increasingly important for Americans to speak other languages. I hope many children follow Holden's example. If Chinese is too tough (and I think it is for many of us), try a different language.

Of course it's easy for me to say all that; my wife, Anne, speaks five languages, and that was enough for someone to think she was a spy. She almost landed in jail once, and it was no laughing matter. During the German occupation of Paris she was writing subtitles for movies. They caught her carrying a briefcase filled with notes in different languages. It was obvious to them that anyone who had papers in all these languages was a spy, so they put her in jail. Fortunately, she was able to prove what she was doing and was released.

Anne often scoffs at the mistakes I make in speaking a foreign language, but she helps me, too.

I don't know how much I did for my country, but I did a lot for myself. I learned about other countries, and I found out that all people have the same yearnings and desires. We need to help one another attain them.

23
ANNE IN ORBIT

My grandchildren love my wife. They call her Oma, which is German for grandma. She showers them with gifts and acts of kindness, but there is another side of her. I've learned in the last fifty years that there are certain times when you have to step aside and let your wife tell the story. For instance, I hardly ever get to talk about what happened after Henry Kissinger returned from his secret trip to China, so maybe I can do it now. You see, the very day Kissinger came back from China, we had a dinner for him at my house with a few carefully selected stars. He had stopped in California to brief President Nixon, who was staying in San Clemente, on his meetings. It was a happy evening, and everyone was eager to hear about his visit to China. After dinner we all gathered around . . .

As I'm dictating this to Grace, my wife walks in. "Kirk, make sure you tell the story right, because you ruined that evening."

"What are you, a spy?" I asked her.

"No, but I will never forget what you did to my dinner and I want it told accurately."

"Would you like to tell it?"

"Yes."

"Okay, go ahead."

Anne turns to Grace at the computer. "It happened like this. Everyone was excited to have dinner with Kissinger. We all ate in a hurry because we were eager to hear about his trip. After dinner, we gathered around the bar and Henry began to mesmerize the audience with his story." Anne looks at me with flashing eyes. "Here's where you came in." She turns back to Grace. "You know that Kirk thinks it's a good evening when he can be in bed for the ten o'clock news. Well, he suddenly flicked the lights, putting an end to Kissinger's talking.

"I was so mad. 'Kirk, what the hell are you doing?' I said. 'Everyone wants to hear the story.'

" 'Honey, Henry's on Chinese time. He should go to bed.'

"I was speechless as the party broke up and everybody left, Kissinger in Sinatra's group. I won't tell you the scene Kirk and I had but that night we went to bed saying nothing to each other.

"At five in the morning the phone rang. Kirk never answers the phone. I picked it up." Anne took a drink of water. "And, Grace, this is how the dialogue went.

" 'Hello?' I said.

" 'This is the Beverly Hills Police Department.'

"Oh my God, I thought, what happened? 'Yes, what's wrong?'

" 'The White House is looking for Henry Kissinger and we know that he was at your house.'

" 'He left hours ago.'

" 'Do you know where he is now?'

" 'No, but I will try to find out.'

" 'We appreciate that and will be waiting for your call.'

"Of course Kirk was still sleeping and I called Sinatra's house. 'Frank?'

" 'Hey, Frenchie, what are you doing up so early?' He always called me Frenchie.

" 'Do you know where Henry is?'

" 'Yes, right here. We're having breakfast.'

" 'Then tell him that his president is looking for him.' "

Anne turns to me and says, "And that's the way it happened."

"Honey, you should have your own television show."

She gives me a look and leaves the room.

Nobody contradicts my wife. And you never know what she's going to do next.

Let me tell you about the kind of girl I married. When Anne was pregnant with our first son, Peter, I was about to produce the first movie for our production company — *The Indian Fighter.* The shooting took place in Bend, Oregon. The doctors thought that Anne shouldn't travel.

Diana, my ex-wife, was perfect for a part in the movie, but she was worried about leaving our two young sons behind. So my pregnant wife, Anne, stayed home and took care of Michael and Joel. What a gal.

But she could also be bitchy.

Once we were driving to our home in Palm Springs in two cars. I was driving ahead with the maid and Anne was following in another car with baby Peter and the nanny. I was going too fast and a motorcycle cop pulled me over and started to write out a ticket. I raised my eyes and saw Anne driving past, smiling and giving me a wave. Now that's not nice, is it?

I can never predict what my wife will do.

24
DECISIONS

All of us will make some wrong decisions in life, but we hope that we will make more correct ones. Some of us believe in our first gut reactions to help us decide — I don't. I agree with the French phrase *"Réfléchissez bien avant de vous décider"* — Think carefully before you decide.

When I graduated from high school in 1934 I got an offer for a well-paying job in a wholesale grocery chain. My high school English teacher, Mrs. Livingston, urged me to try to get a college education. It took me one year to decide to hitchhike to college — St. Lawrence University — with $163 in my pocket. I didn't even know whether the school would accept me and I felt guilty as I traveled along the road. Was it right for me to leave my sisters to carry the burden of the household? My answer was yes; with a college education I could repay my sisters for taking care of my mother.

Right decision.

At college I decided to give up my courses in education, which were required for a teaching certificate. Why? I was afraid I might be tempted to take a teaching job because I needed the money. That would end my dreams of being an actor.

Right decision.

During one summer vacation while I was in college I worked in a steel mill in a large city. While there, I met a very attractive girl with rich parents (remember, I was a very poor boy). We had a romantic relationship and she suggested that we get married. I explained that I wanted to finish college and go to drama school in New York and that I wasn't ready for marriage. She said her father would buy us a nice apartment in New York and take care of all our expenses while I was in drama school. He would be glad to take care of everything until I was self-sufficient, she said. Let me tell you, I was tempted. Not to worry about getting a job, no worries about eating. She had a beautiful Cadillac and there was the extra dividend of good sex. What else could a poor Jewish boy want? But deep down inside I knew I would end up as a man without character. Bottom line, I just couldn't do it, and I broke off the relationship.

Right decision.

After finishing drama school in New York, I opted to turn down a major role in a play that would take me on a national tour. I was tempted. The actress in the role of ingenue was very attractive. Instead, I stayed in New York to play a bit part with superstars of the stage — Katherine Cornell, Judith Anderson, Dennis King, and Edmund Gwenn. I didn't even have any lines to say; I was an off-stage echo. I was convinced that it would be better for me to grab the opportunity to work with such stars.

Right decision.

In 1949, after I'd made a few unimportant pictures, my Hollywood agent was overjoyed to secure for me a costarring role with Gregory Peck and Ava Gardner in the big-budget picture *The Great Sinner.* Much to his dismay, I turned it down to play a boxer in the small-budget picture *Champion.* I got an Oscar nomination and became a star. I couldn't resist playing a role that reflected so much of my life. The announcer at ringside, looking at me, says, "From the depths of poverty he became champion of the world!"

Right decision.

In 1953 Billy Wilder offered me the leading role in the film *Stalag 17*. I had seen the play on Broadway, and it had seemed to me too disjointed. I didn't anticipate what the genius of Billy Wilder would do with the script. I turned it down and William Holden played the part. He won an Oscar.

Very wrong decision.

In 1954 I was offered the job of spokesperson for General Electric. The money was good, but I turned it down. Ronald Reagan accepted the job and kept it for eight years. During that time, on behalf of GE, he spoke eloquently to the public on TV. This led to his career in politics. Did I make the right decision?

Yes, because otherwise we might have been denied a president of the United States.

In 1964 I was offered the leading role in a big epic picture, *The Fall of the Roman Empire*. My agent was not happy when I turned it down. Then the producer came back offering more money. I answered that I'd work for less if they would make a script I owned, *Montezuma,* written by Dalton Trumbo. They refused but offered me the astronomical sum of $1.5 million. That would be equivalent to about $20 million today. This was tempting, but I wanted to set up *Montezuma* so I turned down their offer. My agent thought I was insane. The large amount of money would have helped me with my burgeoning production company.

I never succeeded in making *Montezuma* and I forget who played my part in *The Fall of the Roman Empire.* But I remember who played the female lead — the beautiful Sophia Loren.

Another bad decision.

In 1965 I wanted to accept the offer to play the leading role in *Cat Ballou.* My agent talked me out of it because he thought the part was too small. Lee Marvin played the part and won an Oscar.

Bad decision by my agent.

Ben Hogan was a world champion golfer. The studio asked me to play him in a motion picture. In preparation, Hogan would teach me golf for six months. I was then such a gung-ho tennis player that I had no interest in golf. I turned it down. Years later, when I became an avid golfer and found myself trying to hit a ball out of the rough, I thought of what I might have learned from spending six months with Ben Hogan.

Dopey decision.

In 1980 I was the president of the jury at the Cannes Film Festival and I lived at the Hôtel du Cap not far away. Leslie Caron, the talented actress, was a member of the jury. We had our meeting and the committee agreed with me that the winner of the first prize would be *All That Jazz,* an American movie. I returned to the hotel. Meanwhile, without my knowledge, the French head of the festival called a meeting of the committee and convinced everyone that the Japanese picture *Kagemusha* should share the first prize. I was dumbfounded by that decision, which had been made without my knowledge. Furthermore, I was told that in the meeting Leslie Caron had chastised me for not being in attendance.

I was preparing to go to Israel to make a movie, *Remembrance.* The producers had decided to cast Leslie Caron as the leading lady. Instead of discussing it with Leslie, I refused to work with her and forced them to hire an inadequate Israeli actress. The movie was a flop.

Stupid, childish decision.

The day the film festival awards would be presented I learned that Peter Sellers was hiding out at the Hôtel du Cap on the instructions of the studio because they told him he would win the prize for Best Actor for *Being There,* a wonderful movie. Of course, being on the jury I knew that Michel Piccoli was going to get the award. I felt sorry for Peter and invited him and his wife to have dinner with us that evening.

At first I refused to participate in the award ceremony, but Anne calmed me down, insisting that I should present the award. After the ceremony, Anne and I met Peter and his wife at the restaurant Tetou. Of course, Peter felt that he had been duped by the studio, but he appreciated my concern.

The next day they were leaving on a yacht trip and invited us to be their guests. I hesitated because I knew that Peter was having problems with his wife. Anne agreed with me, and we made some reasonable excuse for not going. Reports were that the trip was cut short because of constant arguments, and Peter and his wife returned to London. Shortly after that, Peter died of a heart attack. I felt guilty. Should we have gone on that trip?

I will never know whether I made the right decision.

Yet all of those decisions were minor compared to the greatest decision of my life. In 1974 Anne and I had been married for twenty years when doctors discovered a cancerous lump in her breast. I waited nervously downstairs while the surgeons operated to remove the tumor. My wife was still under sedation when they came into the room to tell me the cancer had spread and the breast had to be removed.

When I recovered from the shock, my dilemma was deciding whether I should wait for Anne to recover in order to discuss this with her or let the doctors operate now while she was on the operating table. The young Kirk part of me shuddered at the thought of mutilating her beautiful body. Shouldn't she play a part in the decision? I didn't know what to do. The older Kirk asked the doctor, "If it were your wife, what would you do?"

"If it were my wife," he answered slowly, "I would do it now. While she's under anesthesia, so she doesn't have to go through all that again."

I decided that it should be done now.

Later, Anne agreed that I had made the right decision.

25
ALMOST DYING

Almost every weekend we drive to our house in Montecito, near Santa Barbara. We love it there. It's quiet, behind us are the mountains, in front are tall palm trees against a blue sky. Today, the sky is crowded with patches of white clouds that look like a herd of grazing sheep. If you stand in the right spot you can glimpse the Pacific Ocean.

We always take Danny and Foxy with us. They like the larger area and spend most of their time madly chasing crows and rabbits. Of course, they never catch one, but they never give up. The house is surrounded by sculpture, but there are no dual busts. I miss them.

Instead, I try to talk to our sculpture of David, made in Israel from pieces of scrap iron. The young boy stands with his body arched, poised to release his sling, which holds a rock. Opposite him is his enemy, the massive Goliath, also made from Israeli scrap iron. Goliath looks very menacing with his shield and spear pointed at little David. I look at them both, posed forever, and say, "David, if you miss, a large part of history will be changed. And you will never grow up to be the sinner you were before you became a hero."

David says nothing and concentrates on Goliath.

"David, are you sorry for the lust you felt when you stood on that parapet like a voyeur and admired the naked Bathsheba bathing?"

Still David ignores me, intent on killing Goliath.

"Aren't you ashamed that you had her husband killed so you could have Bathsheba? He never knew that you impregnated his wife."

I miss talking to my dual busts. Unlike David, they always seem to be listening, even when it's only to laugh at me.

I go on anyway. "If you missed hitting Goliath in the forehead with your sling, he would have killed you at an early age and you would never have written 'The Lord is my shepherd/I shall not want.' Were you afraid of dying that day?"

I keep on talking even though David isn't

listening. "I remember how many times I almost died. I almost drowned when I was eight years old!"

A friend pulled me out of the water. It's strange to me that more than eighty years later I recall the events vividly. A deep trench had been dug for a factory that was being constructed near my house. A work pipe accidentally broke, filling the trench with about five feet of water. Young, adventurous, dumb Kirk placed a pole across the trench and tried to walk to the other side. Of course, he fell off. I was drowning, going up and down in the water. I don't remember feeling panic. I can see, very clearly, two of my playmates running away in fear. I also saw my older friend Wolfie running toward me along the bank. I don't have any recollection of being pulled out of the water, only that I was wet and crying because I feared a spanking for getting my clothes wet. I peed in my pants, but no one could see that in my wet clothes.

In the late 1950s my friend Mike Todd invited me to accompany him in his private plane on a flight to New York. Mike was married to Elizabeth Taylor and they had a house one block away from ours in Palm Springs. He was to receive an honor and he wanted me to present it to him. Liz couldn't go because she had the flu. On the way we would stop off in Missouri and pay our respects to former president Truman, my idol.

I readily accepted, but my wife refused to let me go. She was afraid of private planes.

"Why don't you go commercial?" she insisted.

We had an argument and in a huff I decided not to go. The next morning driving back home we weren't speaking to each other.

Over the car radio, we heard the announcement. The plane had crashed and Mike and everyone else aboard were killed. I pulled over to the side of the road, shocked. My wife had saved my life.

The thought of that incident gives me goose bumps. What an important role Anne has played in my life.

I'll also never forget August 5, 1986. Anne and I entered Chasen's restaurant in Beverly Hills, where they served a famous chili. I was wearing a shirt with a very tight collar. We saw a couple we knew sitting in a booth. I greeted the husband and gallantly leaned over to kiss his wife's cheek. Bending over made my collar tighter and cut off my carotid artery, the artery that brings blood to the brain. I fell to the floor and was carried out of the restaurant. In my groggy state, I asked to be taken home. Fortunately, my wife didn't obey my instructions. Instead, she called the paramedics, and they brought me to Mount Sinai Hospital and en route gave me two adrenaline shots to stimulate my heart. At the hospital doctors inserted a pacemaker.

Never listen to me.

Again, my wife had saved my life.

And then, with a pacemaker monitoring my heart, I was in a helicopter that was hit in midair by a small plane. Two young people in the plane were killed instantly. I was pulled out of the helicopter's wreckage on the tarmac. I survived. Why? Was the grim reaper stalking me?

As if that weren't enough, one day in 1996 I was enjoying a manicure in my den while gossiping with my Israeli manicurist. I told her about the movies I'd made in Israel, then suddenly I started to babble. At first I wasn't aware of it and I tried to tell her about shooting the movie *Cast a Giant Shadow.* Suddenly, I realized I couldn't speak.

The manicurist called my wife, who was playing bridge that afternoon with Barbara Sinatra. She wasn't far away and quickly came home and called my doctor. He advised her not to wait for an ambulance but to bring me to the hospital at once — when you have a stroke, immediate attention is vital. I survived.

Why have I gotten so many reprieves from my inevitable end? Why do so many good people die young and so many bad people live to a ripe old age? No one knows, but I feel that every brush I had with death changed me and made me a better person. I began to think less about myself and more about other people. If I survive a couple more near-death experiences, I might become a very good guy.

I still have a lot of questions but very few answers.

I miss my dogs, who are happily eating their morning meal in the garage. I stretch out on my bed and pick up the book I'm reading, *How We Die* by Sherwin B. Nuland. I read his book *Maimonides* several months ago. I am fascinated by his writing, which is simple and direct.

My wife comes in, bringing my mail

folder. Seeing the title of the book, she exclaims, "*How We Die?!* Why don't you read a book called *How We Live?*" and she leaves before I can think of a snappy retort.

I go back to my book to find Nuland quoting Homer. "The race of men is like the race of leaves, as one generation flourishes, another decays." I close my eyes and think of the leaves on my avocado trees. Many are falling to the ground to give way to new buds. I go back to my book: "There are good reasons that one generation must give way to the next."

I am getting more and more depressed, but I keep reading. My mood changes when I read that a leading physician of the sixteenth century recommended to an aging patient who wanted to regain his health that he try sleeping between two young virgins. I imagine Anne's reaction to that suggestion in my search for the fountain of youth. But my smile doesn't last long when I read, "Old age is a preparation for departure. Far from being irreplaceable, we *should* be replaced." Then Nuland quotes the Frenchman Michel de Montaigne, "Your death is a part of the order of the universe, 'tis a part of the life of the world. Give place to others, as others have given place to you."

I burst out laughing. He died at fifty-six.

He must have given thought to dying at a very early age. When I was fifty-six, I thought I would live forever.

I like what Edgar Guest wrote:

I used to think that growing old was reck-
oned just in years,
But who can name the very date when
weariness appears?
I find no stated time when man, obedient
to a law,
Must settle in an easy chair and from the
world withdraw.
Old Age is rather curious, or so it seems
to me.
I know old men at forty and young men at
seventy-three.

Two thousand years ago, the philosopher Seneca wrote about facing death: "Old men pray for a few more years. They pretend that they are younger than they are. Whenever his last day comes, the wise man will not hesitate to meet death with a fair step."

I have always believed that to retire is to die, but Seneca says, "Is it really so pleasant to die in harness? That is the feeling of many people; the desire for their work to outlast their ability to do it."

Seneca depresses me. He was a Stoic,

which for some reason makes me think he didn't have a sense of humor.

I agree with Richard Bach: "Here is the test to find whether your mission on earth is finished: if you're alive, it isn't."

With my wife, Anne, on our horse sculpture. Our dog Danny is ignoring us; our other dog Foxy doesn't like romantic settings.

Dreaming of far-off places at fourteen years old.

With Anne—our first kiss?

With Burt Lancaster (left) and Sammy Cahn (seated). Burt and I sang Sammy's song *It's Great Not to Be Nominated*.

With my costar, Lana Turner, in *The Bad and the Beautiful*. I wasn't always riding horses in movies.

As Vincent van Gogh in *Lust for Life*.

With my friend Johnny Cash in *Gunfight*.

With former first lady Lady Bird Johnson; Anne is at my right. Luci Johnson read my book *My Stroke of Luck* to her mother.

With Anne and President Ronald Reagan.

Receiving the Presidential Medal of Freedom from President Jimmy Carter.

My son Peter with his dog Shaft, who acted the role of a
ferocious dog in a movie we shot in Yugoslavia.

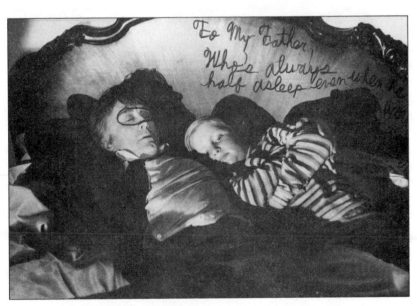

With my son Eric in happier days.

Dancing with my boys (from left, Peter, Eric, Michael, and Joel) in a photograph by Annie Leibovitz.

Eric in the shadow of his father.

With Anne, inaugurating Harry's Haven with our sons Peter, Michael, and Eric, and our friend Jack Valenti.

In Israel with Prime Minister Menachem Begin, who signed the photograph for me.

My son Peter, his wife, Lisa, and their children, Jason, Tyler, Kelsey, and Ryan.

My son Michael with his wife, Catherine Zeta-Jones, and their children, (from left) Carys and Dylan.

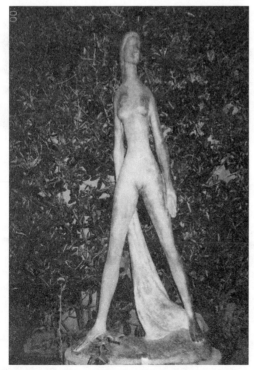

My sculpture of a beautiful nude girl. I bought it in Yugoslavia.

At my second bar mitzvah with Rabbi Wolpe.

At Frank Sinatra's eightieth birthday party, three days after my birthday, in 1995. From left: Gregory Peck, Veronique Peck, Jolene Schlatter, Barbara Sinatra, Frank Sinatra, Anne Douglas, George Schlatter, and me.

Sunday poker at the Sinatras' house.

The object of my affection.

The *real* Kirk Douglas.

Swimming with Danny. See, you *can* teach an old dog new tricks!

Mike Abrums, Anne's and my ninety-two-year-old trainer.

With Anne, breaking the glass at our second wedding.

At the wedding with my two remaining sisters, Ida and Fritzi.

The newlyweds leaving the wedding.

With our housekeeper's daughter, Victoria. I can hear her running down the hall right now.

A fan letter from a child.

Mr. Kirk Douglas July 26 2006
Beverly Hills.ca
Dear Mr. Douglos. My
name is William Johnson.
I like your movies. I
love the one called
Spartocus it is nice.
did you like being
a movie star?
p.s. Is tonycurtis
your best friend?
from William Johnson

I was surprised and honored to learn they named a high school after me.

Giving a talk to the students at Kirk Douglas High School.

On Kirk Douglas Way in Los Angeles. If you live long enough they give your name to lots of things.

My granddaughter Kelsey at her bat mitzvah.

My boys and my grandson at my eighty-ninth birthday dinner.

Me and my boss. Don't let those pretty eyes fool you.

Danny, Kirk, and Foxy, three friends.

26
MAMA'S BOY

Sitting in the Montecito Sun is making me sleepy. I close Sherwin Nuland's book and look at the two warriors, David and Goliath, engaged in a death struggle. They have not moved. I begin to think about the people who helped me in life. My teachers, my wife, my mother — ah yes, my mother. Is she in heaven?

When I was a little boy I slept with the oldest of my six sisters, Betty. I liked that. She would read me stories from Horatio Alger and the Merrywell Boys. They all had such good relationships with their fathers. When I grew a bit older I was transferred to a couch alone, where I read stories of sons with their fathers.

Whenever I reached out for my father I found my mother, but I took her for granted except when I was sick.

Although we were dirt poor, Ma managed to get some eggs and butter and make me "goggle-muggles" — ah, how I loved those concoctions! When I was scared she told me stores about angels. Years later I put those stories in a children's book called *The Broken Mirror.*

As a boy, I worried about my masculinity. How could I ever be as strong as my father? Thank God for my mother. She always told me I was special, that I was a man. Once I sat next to her while she was peeling potatoes. She looked at me with a smile and said in Yiddish, "A boy is a boy but a girl is dreck [shit]." That helped me.

My mother was such a religious woman. Every Shabbat, Saturday morning, I would see her sitting on the porch with a smile on her face holding her Hebrew prayer book. I still wonder what she was thinking.

My interest in religion didn't last long. After I ate my first ham sandwich and God didn't strike me dead, I put religion on the back burner.

Throughout my life, even when I moved further and further from Judaism, I always clung to a thread — Yom Kippur, the Day of Atonement. On that one day I fasted. There was something awe-inspiring to me about that book in which is written "who shall live and who shall die . . . who by fire and who by water. . . ." And who will survive like me.

My interest in Judaism began late in life and was caused by a desire to be spiritually closer to my mother. I began to learn more about my faith by studying with various rabbis. I even dabbled a bit in Kabbalah, Jewish mysticism. Kabbalah has attracted many younger people, not necessarily Jews — Britney Spears, Madonna, Paris Hilton, Demi Moore, and many others. Why so many women, I don't know. I was surprised that Madonna went to Israel for Yom Kippur in 2004!

I am not a pious Jew, but I am intrigued by the fact that Jesus was a Jew and that Abraham took people away from worshiping idols to believe in one God.

I started studying with Rabbi David Aaron in Jerusalem and Rabbi Nachum Braverman of Aish HaTorah. I also connected with Rabbi David Wolpe, a Conservative rabbi of Sinai Temple in Los Angeles.

The Conservative branch is a more up-to-date version of Judaism. I believe in the Law of Mutability — everything changes, nothing remains the same. Orthodox Judaism has a male hierarchy; women play a less important part. In the temple men and women are seated separately, women play no part in the services, and women can't be rabbis or cantors. But in Conservative Judaism, women have an equal role. They sit together with men in the congregation and they participate in all aspects of the services. Conservative Judaism accepts women rabbis and women cantors. There's equality.

Religious rituals change, but one thing is always constant: there is only one God. The final goal of all religions should not be how often you go to the house of worship, but rather that religion should make you a better person.

My four sons were not brought up as Jews because their mothers were shiksas. They respected my Judaism, but I never imposed it on them. All I expected from them was that they grow up believing in one God and that they become caring people. If religion helped them, they could choose any religion.

Only one of my sons, Eric, had a bar mitzvah. He became a Jew.

In 1999, at age eighty-three, I had my second bar mitzvah. (In Judaism life starts over after seventy. So I became thirteen again.) What an event! It happened at the Sinai Temple in Beverly Hills. So many people came to witness this gray-haired man say a young boy's prayer: Larry King, Karl Malden, my son Michael, Catherine Zeta-Jones, Red Buttons, Don Rickles, Roddy McDowall, and, surprisingly, the mayor of Los Angeles, Richard Riordan.

I did it because if there is a heaven, my mother would have liked it. Most of the people present didn't understand the service, but they all understood the speech I made: "I promise to be a good boy." And I've tried to keep that promise.

In 2003, at age ten, my beautiful granddaughter Kelsey announced that she wanted to have a bat mitzvah, the female version of a bar mitzvah. I didn't give it much credibility because a few years earlier she had attended the bat mitzvah of Ivan Reitman's daughter. It was a lavish affair with a tent, an orchestra, and a snow machine pelting the guests with snow. Everyone was impressed, especially Kelsey. I thought her desire for a bat mitzvah was just a momentary whim.

Later I was surprised to learn that Kelsey had studied with a woman rabbi to prepare for her bat mitzvah. She learned all the Hebrew prayers. Yet the most impressive thing to me was seeing this thirteen-year-old girl walking on high heels, obviously for the first time in her life. I guess having a bat mitzvah signifies that you are now a young lady, and she was trying to act like one, without much success, as she stumbled around on her high heels, but she was beautiful. After it was over, I was glad to see that she was barefoot.

That she grows up to be a Jewish woman is of minor importance to me. The main thing is that she grows up to be a good person. And I think she will.

27
THE DANGERS OF CELEBRITY

Paparazzi are freelance photographers who take candid pictures of celebrities for publication. The more sensational the photo, the more a paparazzo is paid. The word *paparazzi* comes from the name of a character in *La Dolce Vita*. Federico Fellini first saw the name in the novel *By the Ionian Sea*.

Paparazzi are a constant annoyance and even a danger. I will never forget watching a tennis match with Princess Diana from the Royal Box at Wimbledon. We ate strawberries and cream. Diana was so charming, modest, and vulnerable. It was hard to believe that this young girl and her escort were killed in their limousine while trying to evade paparazzi chasing after them in cars and motorcycles through a Paris tunnel. The world mourned and this event turned a spotlight on the paparazzi, but it didn't slow down their activity.

When a pack of paparazzi followed Reese

Witherspoon and blocked her from entering her home, she filed a police report for false imprisonment.

While driving home in broad daylight, Lindsay Lohan was stalked by a paparazzo in a minivan. In a desperate attempt to get her photo, he rammed into her car. Fortunately, Lindsay escaped with only cuts and bruises.

A paparazzo was arrested while hiding in the bushes with a camera at the Malibu daycare center where Angelina Jolie and Brad Pitt send their adopted child. A school official said, "Some of these paparazzi are like predators who will recklessly take and sell photos of innocent children for money."

Certain fans can also be more than obnoxious. One of them, posing as a photographer standing along the red carpet, spewed water from a fake microphone on Tom Cruise. Tom handled it very diplomatically. Another female fan in a nightclub hit Leonardo DiCaprio with a bottle. The reason for her rage was never disclosed.

In 2004 our daughter-in-law Catherine Zeta-Jones had an experience that was almost tragic. My wife and I began to receive handwritten letters threatening Catherine. We kept the letters but decided not to say anything so as not to alarm Cath-erine, who was making a movie in Holland.

Then the tone of the letters changed drastically. They warned that Catherine would be killed. Apparently, the sender was in love with my son Michael and wanted to get rid of Catherine.

We quickly called the sheriff, Lee Baca, who instructed us not to open any other letters that came in. Hoping to get finger-prints, he asked us to wear rubber gloves when handling them.

The letters kept coming. One was ad-dressed to Michael's old apartment and exactly described the floor plan of the hallway leading to the apartment. The return address on the envelope was mine, and since Michael had been long gone from that apartment, the letter was "returned" to me. We were still wondering whether we should discuss the situation with Michael when Catherine received a personal phone call in Amsterdam from the perpetrator, a woman, threatening to have her killed.

Can you image how that made Catherine feel?

The police traced the call. They discovered that a telephone card had been used and quickly found out where the card had been purchased. After finding the culprit's finger-prints, they arrested her, an attractive young girl.

She is now in prison under psychiatric observation. Michael and Catherine, with their two children, Dylan, five, and Carys, three, have moved to Bermuda, Michael's mother's home. They are far away from the paparazzi and stalkers, but they are still wary of them.

28
THINKING ABOUT DEATH

My friend Ray Stark, who used to be my agent, had a wonderful sense of humor. Once, during a meeting at my house, my butler, Kurt, a bald-headed German, brought in some coffee. He stood erect and almost clicked his heels when he left, whereupon Ray said, "I thought I told him to wait in the submarine."

Sometimes Ray's sense of humor backfired. In London he was producing the picture *The World of Suzie Wong*. Nancy Kwan, Marlon Brando's girlfriend, played the lead. Nancy became upset over something, so Brando called Ray to speak on her behalf. Unfortunately, Ray assumed that it was me calling, playing a joke on him and talking like Marlon Brando. He said a lot of things he shouldn't have said and Brando hung up. Suddenly, it occurred to him that maybe it *was* Marlon Brando. In a panic he called me and found out the truth.

The greatest sadness in Ray's life was when his son Peter committed suicide by jumping out of a window in New York. Peter was thirty years old. What was in his mind, that he thought death was preferable to life? At the time, Ray was in California, and I went with him to New York. The body was at the police station because suicide is a criminal act. In the words of the philosopher Immanuel Kant, "Suicide is not abominable because God forbids it. God forbids it because it is abominable." We claimed the body, then we went to make funeral arrangements.

The coffin salesman described his products in a low, unctuous tone. The coffins were strong, made of metal. They looked like safes on the outside, but inside they were soft white velvet. The salesman tried to sell Ray a coffin that would be "worthy of your son." Of course, it would be the most expensive coffin. Now, I'm not against coffin makers — they're just trying to make a living — but this disgusted me. I asked to see a simple coffin. The salesman glared at me.

When a loved one dies, many people feel that they should show their love by buying an expensive coffin — a coffin made of heavy metal, watertight. Are they afraid that dust might get in? Years ago people were buried in shrouds, and they still are in the Middle East. What happens when poor people try to display their affection by buying an expensive box they can't afford? They go into debt.

When I visit Eric's grave, I pass two elaborate metal coffins placed above the ground. One contains the remains of the billionaire Marvin Davis; the other is reserved for his wife. All the other coffins in the cemetery are buried in the ground or placed in sealed vaults. It makes me think of the pharaoh king being buried in such an ornate sarcophagus.

I was not surprised to see Pope John Paul II in a simple wooden casket. I have instructed that when I die, I also be buried in a simple wooden coffin, not one of metal and not waterproof.

Maybe I should go into business with a big lumber company and make very simple coffins that all people can afford. We must be weaned away from the concept of having a coffin that protects us from the earth. A coffin should allow the body to come in contact with the earth. Dust to dust.

Ray Stark died at eighty-eight. I admired

the dignity of his death. He put his house in order. He took time to select works of art to give to all of his close friends. I cherish the Henry Moore bust that now sits in my living room. He even made arrangements for his four dogs to be taken care of. In contrast, a friend of ours had been divorced from his first wife for many years. They hated each other. He married someone else and eventually he died, but since he had never liked to talk about death, he hadn't changed his will. His first wife, whom he hated so much, got everything.

Don't let that happen to you. No matter how old you are, it's not a bad idea to think about death. It is inevitable. You cannot avoid it. And it's true that part of living is how you deal with dying.

I was quite young the first time I really thought about death, when I read this poem by John G. Neihardt:

Let me live out my years in heat of blood!
Let me die drunken with the dreamer's
    wine!
Let me not see this soul-house built of mud
Go toppling to the dust — a vacant shrine.

Let me go quickly, like a candle light
Snuffed out just at the heyday of its glow.

Give me high noon — and let it then be
    night!
Thus would I go.

And grant that when I face the grisly Thing,
My song may trumpet down the gray Per-
    haps.
Let me be as a tune-swept fiddlestring
That feels the Master Melody — and
    snaps!

In my youth, that poem fascinated me. It provided such a dramatic view of death. Coralie Hughes, Neihardt's granddaughter and trustee of the Neihardt estate, gave me permission to use the poem. She wrote, "The poem expresses Neihardt's view of death from the perspective of a young man. As my grandfather grew older, he changed his opinion of death from 'the grisly thing' to that of the last great adventure." And now, here I am, an old man and I agree completely. Death is no longer the grisly thing. It has turned out to be an adventure. At ninety you no longer can do much for yourself, but you can certainly do a lot for others. Helping others is now my great adventure.

Age does not deal kindly with old movie stars. If you live long enough, you are permitted to pass on to the other side without much fanfare. I might get a big obituary but little more. But if a movie star dies young, that's another thing. They have faced "the grisly thing." Now they exemplify the "tune-swept fiddlestring that feels the Master Melody — and snaps!" James Dean will forever be remembered as a tormented teenager. Marilyn Monroe will always remain sexy and vivacious. Elvis Presley is still kept alive by his many imitators as well as by his fans' imaginations.

To die young denies you the opportunity to accomplish more in life. You need years to mature and realize that before you leave this earth you should do something to help other people — to do all you can before you finish that fourth circle, old age.

What would have happened to the memory of James Dean if he hadn't died in that awful automobile crash fifty years ago? In his youth he lived in an old apartment on the Upper West Side in Manhattan. Years later the sink needed to be replaced. The tenant wouldn't replace it, though, explaining that "it was James Dean's sink." If James Dean had lived to be ninety, that sink would have been replaced.

I remember listening to Elvis Presley a few months before he died. It was in Hawaii, and Elvis was singing with the same beautiful voice one of my favorite songs, "Are You Lonesome Tonight?" He was still handing out scarves to the girls. Elvis died at forty-two.

Recently someone paid $100 million for the rights to Elvis Presley's name. Would they pay such a large sum if Elvis had died an old man?

As I've mentioned, a group of fans are often standing around Marilyn Monroe's simple vault when I visit Eric's grave. Not a single one of them could imagine an old Marilyn Monroe hobbling along with arthritis or osteoporosis. Like the words of Keats in his poem "Ode on a Grecian Urn," she is "forever young and fair."

Marilyn Monroe never visited France. At the height of her fame, she had to compete with Brigitte Bardot, a beautiful young French sex kitten who made her start in movies in my first film in Paris, *Act of Love.*

In Bardot's short scene in the film, she was bundled up in clothes. It was wintertime, and all you could see was that pretty face. After filming, Anne and I sometimes went to the beach in Lido, Venice. One day I saw a beautiful apparition approaching me in the sand. She had legs that never seemed to end. She kept walking toward me; she was gorgeous. I was astounded when she called out, "Keerk!"

I looked at her.

"C'est moi. Brigitte Bardot." Brigitte became all the rage in France.

Now in the year 2006 Brigitte is seventy-one. She devotes herself to protecting animal rights and is almost forgotten.

This year France has rediscovered Marilyn Monroe forty-five years after her death. Crowds go to see an exhibition of photographs taken shortly before her death. She will forever be thirty-six years old.

Here I am, staggering into my nineties, hard of hearing, hard of seeing, with replaced knees and an impaired voice. If I had died forty years ago, would I be remembered as the Viking dancing across the oars? Maybe.

My son Eric died young at forty-five. I don't appreciate that. He never had the chance to do what he wanted in life. I miss him, especially when I am with my three other sons.

Eric and I did a TV episode together, "Yellow," for HBO's *Tales from the Crypt*. As he was doing a scene, I made a suggestion, and I can still hear his exasperated voice, "Dad, you're not the director."

I miss him. As Shakespeare said, "Golden lads and girls all must,/As chimney-sweepers, turn to dust."

29
Passion Plays

We make movies to entertain, but sometimes movies also teach, and they can influence an audience that now extends all over the world. That is an enormous responsibility. I've produced that kind of movie myself, so I know the responsibility. In 1962 I was very excited about the possibility of making a film of *Seven Days in May,* based on a novel by Fletcher Knebel and Charles W. Bailey and with a screenplay by Rod Serling.

Many governments in the world have been overtaken by military coups. The United States participated in the overthrow of governments in Hawaii in 1893, Cuba in 1898, the Philippines in 1898, Iran in 1953, Guatemala in 1954, and present-day Iraq. Could that happen in America? That was the theme of the book and I wanted Bryna to produce the movie.

Friends advised me not to do a movie

dealing with the subject. Too inflammatory, they said. I was trying to decide when I attended a luncheon at Vice President Lyndon Johnson's residence in Washington. It was a buffet, and as I carried my heavily laden plate to the table, President Kennedy came up to me. I was astonished when he asked, "Kirk, are you going to do a movie of the book *Seven Days in May?*"

I thought, oh boy, here it comes, but I took a deep breath and said, "Yes, Mr. President, I'd like to."

His answer almost made me drop my plate.

"Kirk, I think that would make a really interesting movie."

After that, I could hardly eat, I was so excited.

Fredric March played the president, brilliantly. There were two other good roles, a hero and a villain. I asked my friend Burt Lancaster to choose either role if he was interested. He played the villain — the military officer who tries to overthrow the government — and I played the hero who tries to stop him. It was a provocative film but a responsible one, I thought. It was obviously conjecture, not presented as fact. Everyone who saw the picture took it in that spirit.

Mel Gibson made a movie, *The Passion of the Christ,* that was supposed to offer a new perspective on the death of Jesus, and it was all that anyone in Hollywood and a lot of other places could talk about in early 2004. In his film Mel Gibson depicted Jews as killing Jesus. I want my grandchildren to see the film when they are older.

The movie is an updated version of what in the Middle Ages was called a Passion play, a street drama typically put on during the Lenten season before Easter. The Passion play dramatized the last agonizing hours of Jesus's life and it often riled Christian mobs to go on murderous rampages against the Jews. Hitler wrote:

> It is vital that the Passion Play be continued. For never has the menace of Jews been so convincingly portrayed as in this presentation of what happened in the times of the Romans. They will see in Pontius Pilate, a Roman racially and intellectually superior; there he stands out like a firm, clean rock in the middle of the whole muck and mire of Jewry.

Is it possible that Mel Gibson agrees with

what Hitler said about the virtues of the Passion play?

Early on Saturday morning, July 29, 2006, a car was speeding erratically at over eighty miles per hour. Mel Gibson was the driver, and he was arrested and charged with drunk driving. The deputy's report stated: "The star was abusive, shouted anti-Jewish slurs, attempted to escape from custody, and boasted that he 'owned Malibu.'" When he was handcuffed he reportedly said, "You're going to regret you ever did this to me" and called a female officer "sugar tits." He looked at another officer and reportedly asked, "Are you a Jew? The f — Jews are the cause of all the wars."

I'm a Jew, an American Jew. Mel, do you think that we Jews started the war that ended in the Holocaust? It's hard to excuse an anti-Semitic tirade because of a half-empty bottle of tequila found in your car, but there is a Talmudic saying, "When wine enters in, the truth comes out." In Latin they say the same: *In vino veritas.* That's one thing that almost everybody agrees on — when you're drunk you tell the truth.

Mel's subsequent apologies for his actions sounded too pat and not remorseful, like something scripted by a publicity agent trying to put Mel's best foot forward. One apology was like an afterthought — *Oh yes, the Jews.*

He was invited, or his publicity department arranged for him, to speak at Yom Kippur services at a temple. Would a rabbi permit an obvious anti-Semite to talk on this holy day? I don't think so. But from Mel's point of view, it was perfect. He could pretend to fast with other Jews on that day of atonement, he could utter in English the prayers that are written in Hebrew: "Who among us is righteous enough to say I have not sinned? We have confessed, we have gone astray, we have sinned, we have trespassed."

An actor of Mel Gibson's talents could have been a hit, but he finally decided against it. Then he tried to apologize again in an October 2006 interview with Diane Sawyer — without much success, I think. Mel is too good an actor; he should have done better.

In the months before *The Passion of the Christ* was publicly released, it was screened for industry movers and shakers and carefully selected critics. Mel cleverly created a fantastic buzz of publicity about the picture. In a 2004 TV interview with Diane Sawyer, he said, "They are trying to put a wedge between me and my father." Mel's father is

Hutton Gibson, a well-known anti-Semite who has espoused views much like those who believe that *The Protocols of the Elders of Zion* is authentic. This spurious manuscript was created by Russians and printed in Paris in 1905; it talks about a worldwide plot by Jews to take over the world. It was debunked as a forgery long ago, but Hutton Gibson "outlined a conspiracy theory involving Jewish bankers, the US Federal Reserve and the Vatican, among others," as reported by an Australian newspaper, *The Age,* on February 19, 2004.

Children are influenced by their fathers — they often look up to them and idolize them. My relationship with my father was obviously much different. We were never close, although I tried to be. We never had any talks about his thoughts and what he expected from me.

How much influence did Mel Gibson's father have on him? Hutton Gibson denies the Holocaust. Denying the Holocaust is a new form of anti-Semitism, and it is a crime in Germany and Austria.

David Irving, a successful English writer, was tried for this offense in an Austrian court in 2006. Though he pled guilty, he appeared in court carrying one of his books, *Hitler's War,* which denies the Holocaust.

Irving recanted some of his positions. "I made a mistake when I said there were no gas chambers in Auschwitz," he told the court. He also expressed sorrow "for all the innocent people who died during the Second World War." Too late. The court found his apologies insincere and he was sentenced to three years in an Austrian prison.

There are many people, though, who still deny the Holocaust.

Before seeing *The Passion of the Christ*, I was very interested in the comments being made about it. I read all the interviews Mel did in prerelease publicity. He claimed to have made this picture based on the Gospels. Of course, the Gospels — Matthew, Mark, Luke, and John — were written many years after the death of Jesus, and the versions differ. Recently — well after Mel's film was released — fragments of a version of the Gospel of Judas were discovered in Israel. In this version Jesus asks Judas to betray him.

Mel also used as his source the "visions" of Anne Emmerich, an eighteenth-century German nun. After her death, a book was written describing her vision "of the suffering of Jesus before he was crucified." The Vatican has never confirmed the validity of her visions. The fact is, she was an anti-

Semite who believed that Jews ritually sacrificed their own children.

Mel is a Catholic. Although he does not recognize the pope, he nonetheless tried to engage the Catholic church in his publicity ploys. His company claimed that the movie conformed to the Catholic bishops' guidelines. This claim was contradicted by Dr. John T. Pawlikowski, a priest and a professor at the Catholic Theological Union in Chicago, who warned after reading Mel's script that it had "real potential" for reviving Christian anti-Semitism. In a paper, *Christian Anti-Semitism: Past History, Present Challenges,* Dr. Pawlikowski wrote, "The main storyline [of Mel Gibson's script] presents Jesus as having been relentlessly pursued by an evil cabal of Jews. . . . This is precisely the storyline that fueled centuries of anti-Semitism within Christian societies. This is also the storyline rejected by the Catholic Church at Vatican II in its document *Nostra Aetate* and by nearly all mainline Protestant churches in parallel documents."

A few days before the film's opening, I got an invitation to view it at Mel's office at ten in the morning. I declined and saw it a few days later along with everybody else.

Sitting in the theater waiting for the film to begin, I couldn't help but think that I was probably the only living Jew who had played a character who was crucified in a movie, in *Spartacus.*

At one time, while shooting a film in Rome, I lived in a villa near the Appian Way. Very often, in the evening, I would take a walk along that famous road. Many of the stones that were used to make the road are still there, and ancient pieces of Roman statuary lie on each side of the road. Sometimes I'd close my eyes and imagine I could hear the sound of Roman legions marching along this route. Of course, all evidence of crucifixions is gone. What a cruel period in history!

The lights dimmed and Mel's movie began. I saw Jesus — a well-built, handsome young man with a finely chiseled nose, unlike the hooked noses of the other Jews depicted on the screen. (The movie later got an Oscar nomination for makeup — the "really big noses," as Frank Rich of the *New York Times* put it.)

I was dumbfounded by the violence: unbearable, distasteful, sadomasochistic. It was almost like a porn film, with a nearly naked man being whipped until the blood flowed. The gore was shot from every conceivable angle. Of course, the Jews were depicted as laughing at the plight of their fellow Jew. The audience around me reacted in many different ways. Some people were appalled. Some cried. Others clearly enjoyed the violence.

I've got to hand it to Mel. He was a genius at taking advantage of the controversy and the resulting free publicity. He made it a must-see picture while also generating a tie-in book, a soundtrack recording, and a commemorative "crucifixion nail" — must-have items for the Easter season.

The movie got mixed reviews. Anna Quindlen, who is Catholic, wrote in *Newsweek:* "Mel Gibson's gory cinematic take on the crucifixion is a new wedge issue, religiosity, not to be confused with faith." She concluded, "I've got the uncomfortable feeling that Mel Gibson was trading on God for personal gain, the modern version of thirty pieces of silver."

In the years to come, this movie will be shown over and over again — in America, in Europe, and in places in the world where people couldn't care less about Jesus and where they hate the Jews. What will be the end result of this Passion play on film?

What will my grandchildren think when

they see it? One day I hope Mel Gibson will ask himself — was it worth the money?

30
SECOND WEDDING

May 2004 marked the fiftieth anniversary of my wedding to Anne. I promised to marry her again because our first try was almost a catastrophe.

The first time we got married was in Las Vegas in 1954 while I was making the film *20,000 Leagues Under the Sea.* We rushed off after a full day of shooting to get married in the hotel suite by a justice of the peace called Honest John Lytel.

The phone rang — Danny Thomas was delaying his show for us. Anne felt nervous and when Honest John prompted her, "I, Anne, take thee, Kirk, as my lawful wedded husband," Anne, though she spoke English very well, repeated what she thought the justice of the peace had said: "I, Anne, take thee Kirk as my *awful* wedded husband." She thought it meant awe-inspiring, but the titters almost stopped the ceremony. We finished and went down to see Danny —

not too romantic. So I promised to give her another wedding one day. It took me fifty years.

When we were making the plans for our second wedding, Anne surprised me by saying, "I want to convert to Judaism."

"Honey, after all these years, why would you want to do that?"

"You have been married to two shiksas," Anne answered. "It is time for you to marry a nice Jewish girl."

Most Jewish mothers do not tolerate their children marrying gentiles. Some of them go as far as to consider a child dead for marrying outside of the faith. Not my mother. I married twice and brought each of the shiksas home to meet my mother. She greeted them graciously and made them feel comfortable. I appreciated that.

A joke:

A telephone rings in a house, and the mother answers. It's her daughter.

"Mama," she says, "I'm engaged."

"Mazel tov!" the mother shrieks excitedly.

"You have to know something, though, Mama. John isn't Jewish."

The mother is quiet.

"Also he's looking for work. At the moment, though, we don't have any money."

"That's no problem," the mother says. "You'll come live here with Papa. We'll give you our bedroom."

"But where will you stay?"

"Papa will sleep on the couch in the living room."

"And what about you, Mama?"

"About me you don't have to worry, because as soon as I get off the telephone I'm jumping out the window."

My mother would never have thought of jumping out the window. If she disapproved, she still loved me, her only son, too much to ever let me know.

Anne began her studies with our rabbi. Judaism doesn't proselytize. Rather, Jews make it difficult to convert. After talking to her for a short time, Rabbi Wolpe said, "You don't have to convert to Judaism. You believe in God, you pray to Him — that's enough." Nevertheless, Anne insisted. She became alarmed, though, when he told her she had to immerse in a ritual pool as part of the conversion ceremony.

"All the way?" she asked.

"Completely!"

"What about my hair?"

She overcame her hair concerns and ducked into the water. When she bobbed up she was a Jew. She was ready to be married again.

The first ones down the aisle of the rose garden at the Greystone Mansion were our children and grandchildren. Tyler, eight years old, was clutching the coat of his younger brother Ryan, who was determined to be the first at the chuppah, the ceremonial canopy used in Jewish weddings. Three hundred people, including Lauren Bacall, Nancy Reagan, Tony Curtis, Karl Malden, Merv Griffin, Sidney Sheldon, Red Buttons, Don Rickles, Angie Dickinson, and Jennifer Jones, turned their eyes toward Anne as she came down the aisle. She looked beautiful in a pearl gray gown. The orchestra played "Love and Marriage."

I pushed past the photographers and walked down from the opposite end of the aisle to meet her. I threw away my cane and put my arms around her in a tight embrace. The music changed to "I'm in the Mood for Love."

As we approached the chuppah, a canopy of roses, we saw Rabbi Wolpe waiting there to marry us. He whispered, "The first time you were married I wasn't even born."

Rabbi Wolpe has a great sense of humor, and when the crucial moment arrived, he had a twinkle in his eye: "Now I am going to say something that I have never had the opportunity to say before: 'Will Kelsey, the granddaughter of the bride and groom, bring up the wedding rings?' "

After everyone laughed, it was time to break the glass. This is part of the Jewish ceremony. On the soft ground lay a glass wrapped in a napkin. I stomped down on the glass. It sank in the earth but did not break. I tried again. No success. The audience began to giggle. I took my cane and smashed the glass. People broke out in laughter and applause.

The rabbi then said,

There are many explanations for why we step on a glass at the end of a wedding. It is a memory of difficulty amidst joy, the trials of history as well as the inevitable difficulties that any couple will face. But there must be a reason why we break a glass and not a plate or some other object. Perhaps it is because we can see through a glass, but once it is broken, everything changes. We can never see through it the same way. Once you are married, everything looks different. Now we see not only through our own eyes, but through each other's eyes. You know through half a century how everything you see has changed. You have been given the gift of new vision of second sight.

After the ceremony, the audience drifted down to the reception area for food and drinks. It was my turn to take center stage.

A month before the wedding, at a charity dinner that Anne hosted for Women's Cancer Research, I sat next to Linda Thompson, the wife of music producer David Foster. After a few drinks, I told her of a song that I'd composed.

"Words and music?" she asked.

I answered, "Of course," and had the chutzpah to lean over and sing the song in her ear, against the background of lively dinner conversation.

"Not bad," she said effusively and turned to her husband. "David, Kirk has written a song that I think he should sing at his second wedding."

"Great," David answered. "Come to my studio and we'll make a record of it."

Things had moved so rapidly I could only stutter in reply.

A week later I was on my way to his beautiful home and studio in Malibu. I was nervous because by then I'd learned more about David Foster. He has won fourteen Grammy Awards and has been chosen Producer of the Year three times. He is a successful songwriter and pianist. When I arrived at his luxurious studio I learned that he has produced records with almost all the superstars — Michael Jackson, Paul Mc-Cartney, Neil Diamond, and many, many others.

I sat down next to him at the keyboard, feeling even more intimidated to hear that in the adjacent studio a crew was waiting for him to create the background music for a song that Celine Dion had just recorded in Las Vegas.

David made me feel very comfortable and I sang the song while he improvised a tune on his keyboard. It didn't take long, and it was very pleasant. Finally he said, "Well, that's it, Kirk. We got it and I like it."

A few days later I received several CDs of our work together, which he insisted I play at the wedding.

So while our guests were noshing and drinking in a large open area, two big wooden doors opened and the sound of trumpets announced the arrival of the newlyweds. We walked in and greeted our friends. After the applause died down, they

played the recording of a poem and the CD
of the song I had written for my wife, accompanied by David Foster's music.

First I recited my corny poem:

Does fifty years together
Seem so long ago to you?
The older the violin, the sweeter the music.
It is often said, and it's true.

To me, it seems like yesterday
We met in gay Paree.
Now Paris is sad, but I am glad
You chose to marry me.

I had the audacity to sing along with the
CD loudly playing:

When you call me angel,
I begin to sprout wings.
Just whisper darling,
Hear how my heart sings.

I melt when you're near me,
Like snow on a sunny day.
Dissolve when you touch me,
Like teardrops kissed away.

And if you ever leave me,
I will follow you and cry,

Please, please, stay with me
Until the day I die.

And then I spoke:

I am not a singer of songs,
That is plain to see
All I am trying to say is please stay in love
    with me.

I dared to end with:

And if you ever leave me
I will follow you and cry
Please stay in love with me,
Until the day I die.

I was surprised — it was well received. One woman, a drink in hand, said, "Kirk, you made all the husbands here look like shit."

During our fifty years together, I was not always the perfect husband. Did I make up for it with a second wedding? It didn't hurt.

31
HATE

In my dressing room I look at the pictures of Eric on the wall. One of the pictures was taken when Eric was about ten years old; he's cradling Anne's poodle Teddy. Above that is a photo taken in New York when I was shooting *The Brotherhood*. I wore a mustache for my role, the makeup man put a similar mustache on Eric, and we both glared out at the camera. My favorite picture is of the two of us lying together, Eric's arm around me. Eric signed it in his childish scrawl: "To my father, who's half asleep, even when he's half awake."

My head is filled with thoughts of Eric. I leave the dressing room and throw myself onto my bed. My two dogs sitting on the floor watching me seem to know that I'm sad. I give the signal that I use with all of my dogs — a slap on the bed. Danny jumps up beside me, Foxy jumps up onto the foot of the bed, and we all lie together very still.

To have a son die before you do . . .

To dispel my dark thoughts I press the remote control and look for a cheerful comedy program.

I gasp. The screen is filled with a video of an enraged mob in Falluja, Iraq. People are swarming around a burning vehicle that carries American passengers. Later, witnesses said that the Americans were still alive when one boy came running up with a jug of gasoline. Young men, their faces covered with scarves, hurl bricks into the blazing vehicle. Another group yanks out a smoldering body and rips it apart. A chunk of flesh is tied to a rock and hung on a bridge girder over the Euphrates River for all to see. A young boy grinds his heel into a burned head. I am appalled that so many young children participate in such atrocities.

Did my grandchildren see this video? I hope not.

My memories of Israel are pleasant: children playing soccer on the field that I gave them . . . a Palestinian graciously choosing a banana from a fruit stand, peeling it, and handing it to me because we restored a playground for some Palestinian children . . . lunches with Teddy Kollek, the mayor of Jerusalem, always in Arab restaurants since he couldn't stand Jewish food . . . watching Jews praying at the Wailing Wall . . . young people singing and dancing in Tel Aviv . . . having lunch with Chaim Topol, a famous Israeli actor, in a Tel Aviv restaurant.

What is happening in the world? What is the source of the rivers of hate that are causing so much suffering? It is not money but hate that is at the root of evil everywhere and of every kind: jealousy, ignorance, pathology, racism, bigotry, political hostility, religious intolerance. For some people, as President George W. Bush once put it, "hate is a faith," a mentality whereby the end justifies any and all means.

Scientists explain that hate emerges from the amygdala (I can write it, but I can't pronounce it), the area of the brain responsible for certain kinds of reactions and emotions. This area is the size of a grape, situated deep inside the brain at about the level of the temple.

In prehistoric times, when one Neanderthal man hated another, he might have picked up a boulder and smashed the other man's head. Now hatred has more sophisticated tools. Still, much remains the same.

Suicide bombers? Airplanes as weapons? These are not new. In World War II, kamikaze pilots chose death by crashing airplanes, loaded with explosives, into warships. They, too, considered themselves martyrs, but they were diving at warships — military targets. Today suicide bombers blow themselves up at pizza parlors, restaurants, office towers, or bus stops and kill civilians — men, women, and children, often their own people.

Is hatred ever justified? I think so, sometimes. We should hate evil. It takes a strong emotion to force us into action. Nobel Peace Prize winner Elie Wiesel said, "The opposite of hate is not love, it is apathy."

We should teach our children the words of Anne Frank, a Jewish girl who lived for two years in hiding, knowing that many people wanted her dead simply because she was a Jew. She ultimately died in the Bergen-Belsen concentration camp. She wrote in her diary, "I still believe, in spite of everything, that people really are good at heart." The importance of Anne Frank's lesson should never be forgotten.

This is one of my favorite stories of love in action in the middle of strife. It fills me with hope and inspires me to find the goodness inside myself and to reach toward another person with loving-kindness.

Near the Iraqi city of Kirkuk, a girl named Bayan Jabar was born with the arteries of her heart reversed. Iraqi doctors didn't know what to do. An American doctor on hand told them to call the Israelis, and they did. Over the phone, an Israeli doctor instructed one of the Iraqi doctors on how to keep the baby alive until she could be airlifted to Israel.

In the days of Saddam Hussein such collaboration would have been impossible. This tyrant sent millions of dollars to reward families of suicide bombers who murdered Israelis, while he kept his own medical system in the dark ages. But with the American forces in Iraq, new bridges have been built between cultures.

On November 21, 2003, Bayan and her parents flew from Baghdad to Amman, Jordan, and then drove to Israel, where the week-old baby was operated on at the Wolfson Medical Center in Holon. After the delicate ten-hour procedure, which had to be performed within two weeks of birth or the baby would have died, the Israeli doctors reported that the operation was successful and the baby's heart was working normally.

Bayan's parents were delighted. Her father, Jesem, said, "I never imagined that I would ever come to Israel. I was told in the past that Israel is a bad place, but now I see that people here are good and everyone wants to help."

Dr. Moshe Mashiah, the director of the Wolfson Medical Center, said that as a Jew who was forced to flee Iraq in 1951, he is very excited by the possibility of aiding the Iraqi infant. He told the Associated Press, "I hope the surgery will be successful and that this baby girl will serve as a bridge between the two peoples."

Maybe this girl, together with my grand-children, will help to end the cycle of hatred.

32
REAL HEROES

Cameron, Kelsey, Tyler, Ryan, Dylan, Jason, Carys — beware of idols! Don't be too quick to make a hero of someone.

Many moviegoers confuse the stars on the screen with the roles they play. People make actors into heroes. When I look through the fan mail that I've received over the years, I'm embarrassed. But the young must have their heroes.

I have often told the story of picking up a young hitchhiker on my way to Palm Springs. As he got into the car next to me, his eyes widened, his jaw dropped, and he said, "Do you know who you are?"

Yes, I thought, I have written several books to find out who I am. One thing I know, I am no hero.

When I was young, I idolized Charles Lindbergh, as did everybody. When we heard a propeller overhead we all became excited, shouting, "Airplane! Airplane!" as we pointed to the sky. Seeing an airplane was a rare occurrence then. I fantasized that I was Lucky Lindy, all alone up in the sky, eating a sandwich while flying over the Atlantic. He was so modest when he landed in Paris to the cheers of the entire country. I was proud of my fellow American.

The whole country adored Lindbergh. We wrote songs about him. He always seemed calm and unassuming, with his boyish grin.

I was astonished when I learned that Lindbergh was an admirer of Hitler and that he didn't look favorably on Jews. In the newspapers were photos of him with Goebbels, smiling; my idol even accepted an award from Hitler.

His wife, Anne Morrow, was also adored. She wrote many books. I have read some of them, and she was a talented writer. Yet she shared her husband's admiration for Hitler and his antipathy toward Jews.

We were on the brink of war against Hitler; England was tottering. Roosevelt was president and he faced reelection for the third time. Many people thought Roosevelt was too old and were touting Lindbergh as a prospective candidate. What would have happened to our country if Lindbergh, a friend of Hitler, had become president?

Philip Roth speculated about it in his novel *The Plot against America,* in which Lindbergh is elected president. It's a wonderful, chilling book.

Michael Moore is looked on as a hero by many, but he used the platform of the Academy Awards to harangue against the war and our president. This program was beamed all over the world. Many of our troops watched it in Iraq while they were risking their lives to protect us.

Movie people are citizens and are free to voice our opinions, but we must think deeply because we have an unfair advantage — easy access to the media. We can be used by seemingly sympathetic groups and can go in the wrong direction in order to sway public opinion. Mr. Moore's speech did a terrible disservice — he stirred up hatred.

Maybe I'm unfair to Michael Moore, but it's hard to ignore the deprecating remarks he has said about our country. In a speech in Germany, he said, "Americans are possibly the dumbest people on the planet . . . in thrall to conniving, thieving smug pricks. We Americans suffer from enforced ignorance. We don't know about anything that is happening outside of our country. Our stupidity is embarrassing."

You should not say such insulting things about your own country, especially in a foreign country.

I cannot forgive the way he treated Charlton Heston. Even if I don't agree with much of Heston's politics, Chuck is a gentleman. He agreed to have an interview with Moore, and Moore took advantage of the situation and made Heston look foolish. He had been invited to Heston's home and he was treated with courtesy. I winced when I saw the expression on Chuck's face change as he realized that he had been duped. And yet he remained a gentleman and dismissed the interloper with grace.

Compared to Ann Coulter, though, Michael Moore is the nicest guy in the world. In the books that she has written and in her appearances on TV she is vicious. She still thinks Senator Joe McCarthy was a hero. Does she really believe the horrible things she writes and says?

Mark Foley, a Republican congressman, resigned after his salacious e-mails to young male pages were revealed to the public. Ann Coulter, ever a defender of the Republicans, appeared on the TV talk show *Hannity and Colmes* to support Foley. She said he just sent an e-mail asking what a young page wanted for Christmas. Maybe she doesn't know what "horny" means.

How dare Coulter attack the widows of the 9/11 catastrophe? In her book *Godless: The Church of Liberalism, Newsweek* reports, she writes, "I've never seen people enjoying their husbands' death so much." She claims that some of the widows are exploiting the tragic deaths of their husbands for personal gain. Coulter labels one of the widows a Democratic operative, even though she had been a Republican who voted for Bush in 2000. Coulter spends so much time separating the country into left and right and never the twain shall meet. Maybe notoriety and money are Coulter's goals.

A real hero is someone like Rosa Parks, who in my mind we should all try to emulate. She truly changed our world.

The Declaration of Independence states, "All men are created equal" but only white men drafted and signed the Declaration. It took us a long time to correct that — it wasn't until 1920, much more than a hundred years later, that women got the right to vote.

Of my seven grandchildren, two are girls — Kelsey and Carys. You girls will be living in a woman's world. Look at Condoleezza Rice or Michelle Bachelet, who just became the first woman president of Chile, or Angela Merkel, who became the first woman chancellor of Germany. Even Israel had a woman president years ago — Golda Meir. There are about nine other female heads of state. Maybe one of you might become president!

But you don't have to be president or fly over the ocean to be a hero. You can just take a seat on a bus, as Rosa Parks did. At that time, the color line was very strongly delineated. Water fountains, entrances, restaurants, trains and buses, and many other areas were off limits to blacks or were provided separately. Blacks were supposed to sit at the back of the bus, but Rosa Parks refused to move.

I met her years ago at an AFI (American Film Institute) dinner honoring Sidney Poitier. He deserved his accolades. He starred in many wonderful pictures, like *Guess Who's Coming to Dinner*, which was based on the then startling scenario of an African American man falling in love with a white woman and asking her father, played by Spencer Tracy, for her hand in marriage. For me the most exciting part of the evening was meeting the quiet, elegant woman who sat near me, Rosa Parks. She was sweet and soft-spoken, with great humility. I couldn't imagine her refusing to give her bus seat on a bus to a big white thug. She refused even when the driver demanded that she give it up. She is now the first woman to lie in Arlington National Cemetery, and rightly so.

Thousands of Americans paid honor to the body of Rosa Parks in the Capitol rotunda. Senator Barack Obama, an Illinois Democrat who is the only black member of the United States Senate, said, "Rosa Parks did not just sit down on her own initiative. She was part of a movement. She is the mother of the civil rights movement."

I know there are people like Rosa Parks out there all over the world, preparing to do kind, good, and heroic things.

33
READING OBITUARIES

Why do I read obituaries? I've become fascinated with the game of death. I want to know how many people die younger than I am and how many die older. If more people die older, I win. Then there's the obit itself, the summary of a life. It's too bad we all can't read our own obituaries and determine how other people view us.

The one exception to this was Alfred Nobel.

Nobel was the wealthy Swedish businessman who established the Nobel Prize. He had invented dynamite and became one of the world's largest producers of explosives. When his brother died in a test of explosives, a newspaper mistakenly printed Alfred's obituary instead of his brother's. It read: "The Merchant of Death Is Dead. . . . Dr. Alfred Nobel, who became rich by finding ways to kill more people faster than ever before, died yesterday." When Alfred read it and saw that his life amounted to so much destruction and killing, he was devastated. He decided to do something to benefit humanity, and he used his fortune to establish the Nobel Prize for people who do good in the world.

One January morning in 2005, I opened the *New York Times* to read the obituary section when I was stopped by the front page: "Johnny Carson Dead at 79."

I closed my eyes and thought of him. Since he'd retired, he'd become a recluse in Malibu, and I hadn't seen him for years. I had been a guest on his show two or three times, and once I hosted the show. That was a difficult job even though my son Michael was one of the guests. I think the problem was that I was used to acting in movies where the lines were already written for me. This experience gave me new respect for late-night hosts.

For thirty years I watched Johnny Carson, and he was always charming, talented, and likable on the air.

Johnny came to my house several times for dinner. Alcohol was a problem for him and he was variously on and off the wagon. One night at dinner he was on the wagon but, unfortunately, Anne had set the table with aquavit glasses at each place. We had just returned from Norway after shooting *The Vikings* and Anne had brought back a dozen of the glasses. Each glass is V-shaped with a long stem but no base, and you place the empty glass upside down on the table. When it's filled with liquor you have to empty it before you can put it down again. Our guests were intrigued by this unique way of drinking alcoholic beverages. The butler immediately filled up the glasses (Johnny declined) and we emptied them before we could put them down. This happened again before the meal started. Johnny became interested, picked up his glass, and said, "Fill 'er up!" He cared more about the contents, though, so he kept placing the empty glass upside down on the table and immediately picking it up for a refill, over and over. It was a memorable evening and Johnny ended up in the pool fully dressed.

Today I turn the newspaper pages looking for a happy story. I find this one. A twenty-year-old UCLA student — Ahmad Arain, who had been born in Pakistan and came here at an early age — had vanished; he was last seen taking a bus to the campus. Now, six weeks later, his family heard from him. He was in Tijuana, Mexico. Apparently, he'd had a mental breakdown and for a month wandered the streets of Tijuana. A Mexican family found him by the side of the road, took him into their home, fed him, and gave him clothes. The Mexican family didn't speak English and Ahmad Arain didn't speak Spanish. After two weeks he was well enough to contact his family. You can imagine how grateful his parents were for the kindness of strangers.

That story made me feel good.

After lunch, I usually take a walk in the garden — without my cane — to strengthen my aching knees. Next to the roses is a path paved with squares of cement. The squares were all signed by my friends of many years, and I like to bend down and look at them. So many of theses friends are no longer with us: Yul Brynner, Burt Lancaster, Jack Lemmon, Walter Matthau, Natalie Wood, Frank Sinatra, Dean Martin. . . . I look down and step back quickly. I am standing on the president, Ronald Reagan. He signed that square when he was still an actor.

I remember the last time I saw him, climbing the stairs leading to Mike Abrums's gym, a Secret Service agent behind him. We stopped and shook hands; he continued up and I went down. I knew he hadn't recognized me. A few days later, the newspapers published his letter announcing that he had Alzheimer's disease.

I spend lots of time in my garden. I love the roses, so fragrant and colorful — red, white, lavender, yellow. I watch my dogs ferociously pursuing two blackbirds pecking in the garden. They calmly fly away. Danny and Foxy never give up their fruitless pursuit of the birds. Maybe all of us should have goals that we never attain. At home in L.A. my dogs have two unattainable goals — the blackbirds and the cat next door.

I look up at a blue sky with white puffy clouds, unusual in California. Palm trees are gently swaying in the breeze. I am sure that there is a God even though people are killing one another all over the world.

The *New York Times* is still lying on the table. I can't resist — I pick it up and turn to the obituary column:

- Bruce Adams, a senator, died at 77
- Jack Rohan, a basketball coach, died at 72
- Ralph G. Allen, the author of *Sugar Babies,* died at 70
- Jonathan Scharer, a producer, died at the young age of 56

And then one for our side: Frank Thomas, an animator, died at 92. Not bad, one out of five.

The day before I had a home run, with three people over 90:

- Alfred Soloman, 104
- Donald J. Leslie, 93
- George Hetzel Baird, 97

In the obituary column I read something that makes me smile. Robert L. McCullough, an African American civil rights protester, died at 64. When he was 19, he dared to sit at a lunch counter in South Carolina and order a hamburger. He was refused service and arrested for trespassing. This was in 1961, many years after the Civil War — I thought the slaves had been freed. Instead of paying the one-hundred-dollar fine, this American citizen, Robert L. McCullough, chose to do thirty days of hard labor. After serving his time, he said, "My experience strengthened my conviction that human suffering can assist social change."

Because he was short, his friends called him Napoleon. My nickname for him would be Gandhi.

I leave the garden, my Jewish dog Danny following me. Foxy is not around; maybe he is looking for a shiksa dog. It's difficult for Foxy with one blind eye, and he comes back. Apparently, he didn't find a shiksa or she rejected him. He flops down beside Danny, and they both watch me. I start swimming in the pool. This is the exercise recommended by my doctor. After a few laps, I rest on the side of the pool and look up at the two Kirks in steel.

"Hey, you guys, not bad living in Beverly Hills, huh?"

Young Kirk is still smiling as if he's waiting for his picture to be taken. Old Kirk is silent, deep in thought or sleeping. I take another lap around the pool and return to the same spot.

Now young Kirk seems to be laughing.

"What's so funny — my swimming stroke? Wait a few years."

The elder Kirk looks disdainful.

"Do you guys realize what is happening in the world?" Their expressions don't change. "Well, I'll tell you. There's no room for the dead in Sudan. They're digging up old graves to bury the new corpses. Millions of infants are dying from lack of nourishment and AIDS in Africa. Hezbollah and Hamas . . . Arghh, what do you care?"

I push away from them and mutter, "Talking to statues — I can't resist it. People will think I'm crazy."

I continue swimming.

Each day I read in the papers the names of many Americans who have been killed in Iraq. It's sad, but sadder still are the names you don't read about. The people who are wounded, thousands of them, spending their days in hospitals under the care of overworked nurses and doctors. Newspapers and the TV news don't show hospital personnel carrying bloody arms or legs that have been amputated. They deposit these severed limbs in red plastic bags. How many bags have been filled? We will never know. We read the latest statistics: more than 3,000 young men and women killed in action. News reports hesitate to mention that tens of thousands are wounded, their lives destroyed. Young men and women, their lives changed forever.

The poet Siegfried Sassoon remembered them:

Does it matter? — losing your legs? . . .
For people will always be kind,
And you need not show that you mind
When the others come in after hunting
To gobble their muffins and eggs.

Does it matter? — losing your sight? . . .
There's such splendid work for the blind;
And people will always be kind,
As you sit on the terrace remembering
And turning your face to the light.

Do they matter? — those dreams from the
    pit? . . .
You can drink and forget and be glad,
And people won't say that you're mad;
For they'll know you've fought for your
    country
And no one will worry a bit.

I pray that my grandchildren will never
have to face war. I pray that all young
children will never have to go through what
we are going through now.

Let's face it: the world is in a mess.

Why don't old men fight wars? How about
all retirees going to war? What are they doing now — sitting in rocking chairs, playing
golf? We've had our chance at life. How
about trying to make the world a better
place for younger people? Let's do something more worthwhile than sitting around
waiting to die.

We old guys should put to use everything
we have learned. Let's study our school

system. We used to have the highest education standards in the world, but not anymore. Many other countries have surpassed us, even a little country like Poland. Instead of going to war, let's fight to improve our schools, our teachers, and our equipment. Politicians don't listen to people who aren't old enough to vote, but we can make them listen to us. Let's not hesitate to express our opinions to the government by phone calls, letters, and e-mails. Let them know we care. Such an unexpected wave of protest from the old-timers would have an effect — a strong effect. Let's not be concerned only with higher pensions. Let's think about what people will write in our obituaries — did we make the world a better place or did we just make a lot of money?

I'm not against war. I think we should go to war — we should go to war on drugs, we should go to war against doctors who so easily supply addictive medications to young people. I know — Eric found such a doctor. We should go to war against AIDS, against poverty, against famine. There are many worthwhile wars to be fought. Old men and women of the world — let's start!

34
LAUGH, CLOWN, LAUGH

Children's laughter is one of the most pleasing sounds in the whole world. Listen! They are so filled with joy; they have very few things to cry about. I love to hear my grandchildren laugh. It makes me realize that I must not lose my sense of humor and my ability to laugh — especially at myself.

I've never been accused of lacking a sense of humor, but I have to admit that it's hard to find aging funny.

One afternoon when my knees still let me play golf, I noticed some people waiting behind us. I said to my foursome, "Let those old guys tee off first."

"Kirk," one of my friends whispered, "those guys are all about ten years younger than you."

I watched them tee off.

One evening Anne and I were waiting in

line to see a Harry Potter film. As we approached the ticket booth, I was shocked at the price of admission. "Honey, can you believe that? Ten-fifty a ticket!"

My wife answered, "Show them your driver's license — it's half-price for seniors."

I paid the full price.

I never watch my old movies, but one day I turned on the TV and *Cast a Giant Shadow* flashed on the screen. I made that film in 1966. I watched it for a few minutes, then went into my wife's room.

"Honey," I said, "I was a very good-looking guy."

"You think so?" she answered.

"Yes, I just saw myself in an old movie."

"So what happened to you?" She burst out laughing.

Anne never tires of telling my friends that story.

Mike Wallace filmed an interview with Anne and me. They filmed a long shot of us walking along the street with our old dog Banshee. I assumed that the microphone was off and I said to her jokingly, "Why can't a woman be more like a dog?"

Anne didn't think that was very funny, but the microphone was on and Mike used the scene.

There were a lot of reactions. One woman wrote in: "Why can't a man be more like a fire hydrant?"

Anne thought that was funny.

One day I was sitting in the garden enjoying the sun. Anne walked past me carrying a pooper-scooper. I stopped her.

"Honey," I said, "there's something that bothers me."

"What is it?" she asked.

"You always say *I* am going to fix *my* house. *I* must have *my* dogs washed."

"So?"

"Well, honey, it's not *I*, it's *we*. It's not *my*, it's *our*."

She looked at me. "You're right, Kirk."

"Thank you," I said.

"Now," she said, "*we* must clean off the dog poo from *our* garden." She gave me the pooper-scooper and walked away.

For fifty years, I didn't know my wife's age. She never told me, I never asked, and I never looked at her passport. Not long ago, Anne had an accident in the bathroom and cut her head. The doctor arrived and the first question he asked was, "How old is your wife?"

I said, "I don't know," and left the room. I didn't hear the answer my wife gave the puzzled doctor.

Recently, however, the newspapers carried an article about Anne's work on building school playgrounds. It started off, "Anne Douglas, 80 . . ."

Eighty! I was shocked. How could a young man like me be married to such an old woman? There must be some mistake.

During the shortage of the flu vaccine, she asked, "Are you going to get a flu shot or save the vaccine for some old guy?"

My wife finds me funnier as I get older.

Christie Davies, a British sociologist and the author of *The Mirth of Nations,* was asked to name the world's funniest people. Without hesitating, he said, "The Ashkenazi Jews. There's not really anybody in the same league."

I am an Ashkenazi Jew.

Whenever things get bad, it's my Jewish side that saves me. Jews have had to face all kinds of tragedies with compassion and a sense of humor. Sorrow very often precedes laughter. Jewish clowns — comedians — do not have sad painted faces, but they make you laugh. As it says in *Pagliacci:* "Laugh, clown! Even though your heart inside is breaking, laugh at the pain that poisons your heart."

How many comedians are Jewish? Lenny Bruce, George Burns, Don Rickles, Jerry Seinfeld, Rodney Dangerfield, Milton Berle, Charlie Chaplin, Jack Benny, Buddy Hackett, Jon Stewart, Red Buttons, Jackie Mason, Billy Crystal, Jason Alexander, Jan Murray, Shecky Greene, and Sid Caesar — to name just a few. Humor is such an important part of Jewish life.

George Burns was having trouble sleeping. His friend Jack Benny gave him a supronal.

"What do I do with that?" Burns asked.

"You shove it up your ass," Jack said.

"And what happens?"

"It puts you to sleep. All the Europeans use it."

At two o'clock in the morning Jack was awakened by the ringing of the phone. He picked it up. "Yes?"

"Jack, this is George."

"Why the hell are you calling me at this hour?"

"I took the supronal."

"So?"

"My ass is asleep, but I'm still awake."

Charles Lederer was a Jewish screenwriter.

He was visiting a gentile billionaire's mansion in Palm Beach. The hostess was very proud of her porcelain collection. She handed Charles a priceless piece as she continued her conversation. "Of course, some of my friends are Jews, but I don't know why I hate them. I really have no reason."

Charles let the valuable object crash onto the hard marble floor. "Now you have a reason."

A few years ago at our Beverly Hills tennis club, Charles and the pro Jack Cushingham were arguing one day. "Charles," the pro said, "I could beat you at tennis tied to an animal."

"What kind of animal?"

"Anything you can find."

They made a bet and arranged the match for the next day. Anne and I were there with a camera and caught the whole episode. We heard a loud bang as part of the fence came crashing down. Through the opening came an elephant.

Charles, expressionless, insisted that Jack be tied to the elephant's front legs. The game started with Jack serving. As he threw the ball up in the air, the elephant followed it with his trunk. That made Jack very nervous. The game was hilarious but short. It ended when the elephant defecated in the middle of the court.

Philip and Julius Epstein were Jewish writers and identical twins who worked for Jerry Wald, a producer at Warner Bros. Every morning at eleven o'clock Jerry would call his empty apartment and let the phone ring for about five minutes.

"Why do you do that?" one Epstein asked.

"I have a big German shepherd in my empty apartment. When the phone rings he always runs around. I call to give him exercise."

The next morning the Epsteins managed to get into Jerry's apartment, bringing meat for the dog. They waited. Sure enough, at eleven o'clock the phone rang. They picked it up and yelled, "Woof! Woof!"

Mel Brooks knows Jewish humor very well, and his classic musical *The Producers* is a good example of it. Who else could make a hilarious song-and-dance routine titled "Springtime for Hitler"? This is what he wrote about being a Jew:

I may be angry at God or at the world, and I'm sure that a lot of my comedy is based on anger and hostility. . . . It comes from feeling that as a Jew and as a person, I don't fit into the mainstream of American society.

Feeling different, feeling alienated, feeling persecuted, feeling that the only way you can deal with the world is to laugh — because if you don't laugh you're going to cry and never stop crying — that's probably what's responsible for the Jews having developed such a great sense of humor. The people who had the greatest reason to weep learned more than anyone else how to laugh.

Amen.

35
KNEES

My mother often said, "health is wealth." I never thought much about that until I had a problem with my knees. Knees usually cause problems for athletes, especially football players, and I'd never played that sport. But, as I mentioned earlier, the young Kirk was so conceited he insisted on doing his own stunts in movies: walking the oars on a Viking ship on the open seas, doing fancy rope-skipping, twirling guns, juggling, boxing a professional fighter, performing athletic mounts on horses, rappelling down a mountainside, walking on top of a speeding train, and flying through the air on a trapeze (there was a net).

Of course the older Kirk would never take such risks. I guess as we all grow older we take fewer risks. What do we have to prove?

In my late seventies, I had excruciating pain in my knees. I had trouble walking and it was difficult to get out of a chair. I had to give up tennis. Then I had to give up golf, which made me very sad. I cut down on it gradually — from eighteen holes to nine, then from nine holes to three, and finally I had to quit the game completely. I felt trapped. What kind of life was this?

Finally, in the middle of 2005, I visited Dr. Dobkin, my neurologist at UCLA. As usual, I complained about my knees. "I want to get two new knees."

"One knee at a time?" he asked.

"I want to do both knees together. I don't have that much time."

"Kirk," he said, putting his arm around my shoulder, "with all that has happened to you, that's too dangerous. You might not pull through."

I looked at him. "Doc, that would be a better solution than living with my knees."

He laughed halfheartedly and said, "Come on, Kirk, lighten up. Why don't you try a scooter?"

I thought he was joking and told him so. "No," he said, "my next patient uses a scooter with wonderful results. He should be arriving at any minute."

We waited by the elevator until the doors opened and Sheldon Adelson, riding an electric scooter, came out with his wife and an assistant. The doctor told Sheldon he was trying to get me to use an electric scooter, and Sheldon said, "Try this one."

I rode around and felt like a kid.

"How do you like it?" he asked.

"It's great!"

"You'll have one at your house tonight," Sheldon said. He drove his scooter down the hall to the doctor's office with his assistant following him.

His wife turned to me and said, "Kirk Douglas shouldn't ride a scooter, he should ride a chariot!"

Sure enough, that evening the doorbell rang and there was a scooter — unassembled. Before I could put it together, though, I got a letter from my benefactor.

"Kirk," Sheldon wrote, "give the scooter to someone else. I just bought some new-type scooters. I want you to have one." Sure enough, the next night a new scooter, sealed in a cardboard box, arrived.

My son Joel asked me about the first scooter, still unassembled. "Dad, if you don't use it, I could."

So now Joel rides my old scooter to the golf course.

My knees didn't improve and friends suggested a wheelchair. I was appalled at the idea. I countered with my plan to get new knees.

"Are you crazy?" they said. "Operations on both knees at your age? Get a wheelchair!"

A wheelchair? Never!

I discussed it further with Dr. Gold, my internist.

"Kirk, you have been in a helicopter crash," he said. "Two people died instantly; you survived with an operation on your back. You have a pacemaker. You barely survived a stroke. You are eighty-eight years old. Don't do it. And if you succeed in one knee, you will have to go through it all over again for the other. I don't think you could take it."

I shocked him with my reply. "I want to do both knees at the same time." I couldn't go through the process twice.

"Kirk, you're crazy — not many doctors will do both knees at the same time."

Of course Anne was against it and my sons were, too. Anne was frightened at the possibility that I wouldn't survive. I thought a lot about that, but I couldn't stand the thought of having my wife push me around in a wheelchair or riding a scooter. How much time do I have left? It was not an easy decision and I mulled it over for a long time.

I was willing to take the risk — if I died, I'd be out of pain. What worried me was the suffering it would cause my wife, plus I'd be leaving her alone to handle everything. I interviewed many doctors. Anne helped me because she knew that I had made up my mind.

I finally found a doctor at the USC Medical Center, Dr. Vince, who said, "Kirk, I have done both knees on people older than you. You seem to be a healthy sort. I will first do your right knee, your worse one. A team of doctors will be standing by to examine you. If they give me a positive report, I will do the second knee."

I scheduled the operation.

My wife and my son Peter waited anxiously near the operating room. While I was under anesthesia, Anne told me later, the door opened and the head of the medical unit, Dr. Henderson, entered in scrubs.

"Dr. Vince has operated on the right knee," he said with a smile. "The medical team have given the okay, so he's beginning to work on the other knee." He left the room.

Anne and Peter didn't know whether to be happy that he'd finished with one knee or to be frightened that he was operating on the other. They sat there waiting for what seemed to them an unbearably long time.

Finally, the door opened and the doctor announced with jubilation, "It's done! Kirk has two new knees. You can visit him in the recovery room."

With great trepidation they entered.

Anne told me later, "You were conscious, with your eyes open. We were so relieved."

"I'm glad," I said, "because I don't remember anything."

Recovery was a very painful process. I was flat on my back for a week and both knees hurt all the time. I looked down at my throbbing knees, groaned, and felt sorry for myself. The pain was excruciating. I began to wonder whether it might have been better to tolerate the pain of my old knees. Painkillers didn't seem to help much.

I lay in bed moaning about all the things that happened to me: the helicopter crash, the back operation, a pacemaker, a stroke, and now my knees. "Why me?" I muttered out loud, feeling sorry for myself. Then a thought hit me. I came from poverty, got a college education, became a movie star, traveled all over the world, met important people, and made many movies and more money than I ever dreamed of. Why me? Why me? I never ask *that* question. Maybe in life you have to learn to accept the good things with the bad and stop moaning "Why me?"

After I spent a week in bed the pain became bearable and I started working with a therapist. He began with me on my back and stretched my legs in all different directions. Then he put me in a chair and he seemed to repeat the process all over again. It was boring. Little by little, though, I strengthened the muscles in my legs. Finally I could move with a walker. Then I graduated to a cane and hobbled along. Finally, I threw the cane away.

One day I carefully walked around the house in my Bermuda shorts while Danny and Foxy followed me. They could tell that something was different. I was just glad to be able to walk again. Suddenly, Danny gave a sharp bark and raced to the front door with Foxy at his heels. I hadn't heard the doorbell, but I knew that was Danny's way of greeting a visitor. He always barked as if he was ready to chew up whoever came to the door, but as soon as it opened he would wag his tail in hopes of being petted.

The visitor was my friend Jack Valenti. His eyes widened when he saw me standing. "Kirk! Your legs are straight!"

I didn't realize how bowlegged I used to

be. Maybe I'd been in too many Westerns. The knee operation not only straightened out my legs, it also added two inches to my height. I needed them because I'd lost three inches as a result of my back operation after the helicopter crash.

With Sheldon Adelson's permission, I gave my new scooter to the Motion Picture & Television Home before I could be tempted to use it again.

Young Kirk would have sought the double operation immediately. Old Kirk prefers to take things slowly. Of course, I sometimes resent the voice of caution in my head, but it's good to have old Kirk's maturity and wisdom when deciding whether to take a risk.

36
PUT YOUR HOUSE IN ORDER

I had a stroke about ten years ago. My speech is still impaired, but I work on it every day. In the morning, while driving with my wife to the gym, I do speech exercises. At every red light, I repeat the lip and tongue movements. One of these is sticking my tongue out as far as I can and holding it for five seconds. People in the cars alongside us usually look at me strangely, and some of them stick out their tongues in response.

Since the stroke impaired my speech, I talk now more than ever. Sometimes people don't understand me, but I keep talking.

Once a week, I work on my speech with a speech therapist, Tom Heatley. Last week he taught me how to articulate the sentence "The *sh*ade of her *sh*awl was *sh*eer and *sh*iny." But how do you use that in a conversation?

When I have to make a speech I start off

by explaining my stroke. "When you have a stroke . . . you must speak slowly . . . to be understood. I have discovered that when I speak slowly . . . people listen! They think I'm going to say something important." And I laugh with them.

A stroke teaches you to respect the human body. A healthy brain can instantaneously tell your body to wiggle its toes, lift a finger, and say what you are thinking. After a stroke, when you want to express a thought, you have to think about how to move your tongue and lips — things that you used to take for granted.

The psalmist sings, "God, I am awesomely, wonderfully made." When you have a stroke you realize just how true that is.

Tom gives me many exercises to perform and lists of words to read and pronounce accurately — words such as *acrophobia* (fear of heights), *brontophobia* (fear of thunder), and *anuptaphobia* (fear of staying single). I was amused by these names for different fears until I came to one word. I hesitated.

"Go ahead," Tom said. "Say the word."

I just looked at it: *necrophobia* (fear of death and dying).

The word that I dared not pronounce haunted me.

Do I have a fear of death?

Yes, I do.

I remember so vividly the reassurance of my mother — just before she died, she looked at my terrified face and said, "Don't be frightened, son. It happens to everyone."

Yes, we know it happens to everyone, but we think "everyone" means *everyone else.*

I have found one way to avoid the fear of death: busy yourself by putting your affairs in order. It's very important not to be sloppy and leave a mess for other people to clean up. First of all, you have to make a living will. Then you provide for your spouse — that is most important. Then you address yourself to your family, friends, charities, and all the rest. These activities really help you to avoid necrophobia.

Let's face it — you are going to die. I am going to die. We are all going to die. We don't have to dwell on that, but the realization of the finality of death makes life more precious. I feel pain only for people who never get to fulfill life's four circles (childhood, youth, maturity, and old age) — young soldiers killed in a war . . . innocent children who are raped and murdered . . . African children who die from hunger and AIDS.

■ ■ ■ ■

My wife and I made our living wills. We both agree that we don't want feeding tubes inserted just to keep us alive so that we become a burden for others. I believe the quality of life is more precious than life itself. And we don't want the government making family decisions for us.

Not long ago, television and newspapers were filled with the tragic face of a woman who had lived in a vegetative state for fifteen years. I cringed at the fate of poor Terri Schiavo. She never made a living will. Her husband, who became her guardian, said that she'd told him she didn't want to be kept alive by artificial means. The doctors assured him that she was brain dead. After a few years, he gave permission to remove the feeding tube, which would have allowed her a painless death.

Terri's parents, however, interpreted the situation differently and insisted on keeping her alive by reinserting the tube in her body. They gave the media videotapes of their daughter, heightening the conflict and bitterness between them and her husband. He was forced to go to a judge, who believed that no one should interfere with the decision of the guardian and of Terri's doctors.

Then politicians disagreed with the judge's ruling and joined the circus. President Bush rushed to Washington from Crawford, Texas, to sign a bill to keep Terri alive. Catholic priests voiced their opinions to keep Terri alive. The Florida governor, President Bush's brother Jeb, jumped in with an attempt to override the judges. The case went before the higher courts. They all agreed with the first decision that the tube should be pulled.

Meanwhile, Terri Schiavo was in a pitiful state, oblivious to hundreds of protesters in front of her hospital who waved signs that said, "Murderer!" and "Save Terri." Parents pushed children who looked about ten years old across the police line toward the hospital, carrying water for Terri. (Why do these people involve the children?) The TV cameras ground away as the police were forced to gently handcuff the children with tape and drive them to the police station, where they were released.

I wonder, how many of those parents had made a living will?

The tube was finally extracted and after fourteen days Terri Schiavo died what I pray was a peaceful death. All the media pictures of Terri's haunting face disappeared.

The media soon replaced Terri with the face of the dying Pope John Paul II. Years ago my wife and I had a private audience with the pope in the Vatican. With a twinkle in his eye, His Holiness said, "I used to be an actor."

I answered, "Yes, your Holiness, you were also a poet and a playwright."

He chuckled. "That was in my youth."

He gave us each a rosary that he blessed. My wife was speechless, she was so much in awe. It was a memorable experience.

Was God waiting for the pope? Was God waiting for Terri? Is He now waiting for me?

I envy people who are certain that there is a life after death. They expect to live on happily after they die. Think of the young suicide bombers who believe that when they die as martyrs they will be given seventy-two virgins. I don't know what they plan to do with seventy-two virgins. I think that one virgin would be enough for me — well, maybe two.

Why should our egos demand that life continues after death? I think a lot about that. Is there an afterlife? I don't know. Maybe when we die, that's it. Dust to dust.

Of course, if you can believe that life does continue, it's a very consoling thought. Maybe it's good to have faith that there is life after death, but is it true? We have no proof of it.

We should be grateful for the time spent in this world. I have learned to feel more and more gratitude for the good health that I have enjoyed for so many years. We take too many things for granted. We might later find that this world was actually paradise but we didn't realize it. We didn't look around to appreciate the trees, the flowers, the sky.

Maybe this really is the Garden of Eden. I try to believe that.

37
BOTH SEMITES

Again, I'm sipping hot coffee in the garden. It's a chilly morning and I'm wearing a scarf. I put down the newspaper — such depressing news — and I start to walk around the pool. Why do so many Muslims have such hatred for Jews? Arabs and Jews are both Semites, and there was a time when they were friends.

It's too bad. In college, Arabic literature always impressed me, especially the *Rubaiyat* of Omar Khayyam and *The Prophet* by Kahlil Gibran. What beautiful poems. They were my introduction to the glories of Arabic culture and literature.

Omar Khayyam was a mathematician, a scientist, an astronomer, a philosopher, and, thank God, a poet. His quatrains thrilled me.

The Moving Finger writes; and, having writ,
Moves on: nor all thy Piety nor Wit

Shall lure it back to cancel half a Line,
Nor all thy Tears wash out a Word of it.

In a different mood he wrote,

A Book of Verse underneath the Bough,
A Jug of Wine, a Loaf of Bread — and
   Thou
Beside me singing in the Wilderness —
O, Wilderness were Paradise enow!

Kahlil Gibran affected me even more strongly. I've mentioned the beginning of this verse already in this book regarding my wife, Anne:

But let there be spaces in your togetherness
And let the winds of the heavens dance
   between you
Love one another but make not a bond of
   love:
Let it rather be a moving sea between the
   shores of your soul.

What a wonderful thought, so eloquently expressed!

Because of their linguistic abilities, Jews translated many of the intellectual achievements of the Arabic-speaking Muslims into other languages and helped to disseminate their innovations to the rest of the world. Unlike today, Jews and Muslims then worked closely together, in harmony, stressing what they had in common — which is a lot. Maimonides, a Jewish philosopher and physician who lived in Spain and Egypt during the twelfth century, worked closely with Muslims and even wrote many of his essays in Arabic.

I want my grandchildren to know more about the Muslims. I take another sip of coffee, which is still warm.

Jews and Islamist Muslims are now at war with each other, but I am continually amazed by how similar Jews and Muslims are. Both are monotheists. Both revere Abraham. Jews pray three times a day, Muslims five. Jews circumcise their sons at eight days of age, Muslims circumcise theirs at age fourteen.

In their places of worship both traditional Jews and traditional Muslims cover their heads, and all statues and pictures of human beings and animals — graven images — are strictly forbidden. And Jews and Muslims both keep kosher! Like the Jews, Muslims don't eat pork. Like the Jews, they don't eat seafood without scales. Oysters, lobsters, and many other foods that come from the sea are forbidden. In some places in the world, observant Muslims buy their meat at the local kosher market because they know that the meat will not be contaminated by pork.

Why is anti-Semitism aimed only at Jews? Arabs are Semites, too. Yet Joseph Eötvös, a Hungarian nobleman, meant only the Jews when he said, "An anti-Semite is someone who hates the Jews . . . more than necessary."

Long ago both Muslims and Jews had a thirst for knowledge. During the Middle Ages, Muslim thinkers led the world and played a strong role in the rediscovery of classical Greek thought. They were foremost in their knowledge of astronomy and made a significant contribution to the field of mathematics. It was Muslims who introduced our system of numbers and the use of zero. This opened the path to higher mathematics and to the decimal system. If it were not for Muslims, we'd still be writing in Roman numerals. How would you like to write CCCCLXXVIII instead of 478? The contributions that Arabs and other Muslims have made to human history are too great to enumerate.

Muslims believe that Abraham took his son

Ishmael to Mecca to sacrifice him on the black stone in the Kaaba. The Jews believe that he took his son Isaac to Mount Moriah for the sacrifice.

I would like to think that the Muslims are right and Abraham didn't take Isaac to be sacrificed. At cheder (Hebrew school) I didn't like that story. It was the first time that I became angry at God. How could He put anyone to such a test? My anger lingered for some time. But is it so important who was supposed to be sacrificed? Ishmael and Isaac were brothers, so that makes us cousins.

With so many commonalities, I could never figure out why Jews and Muslims kill each other.

Hatred has cost the Muslim people a lot. It has diverted and subsumed their traditions of intelligence and openness to ideas. Some Muslim schools exploit parts of the Koran, using grotesque cartoons to incite hatred of "infidels." Yet, ironically, many Muslims around the world paraded their anger against Denmark because a Dane published cartoons ridiculing Mohammed. The liberal relationship that the Danes had with Muslims has been disrupted.

Many geography books in Muslim countries do not show Israel on the map, only Palestine. The president of Iran, Mahmoud Ahmadinejad, has denied the Holocaust while working to create a new one. Ahmadinejad held a conference in Tehran in December 2006, which was attended by some sixty scholars from thirty countries. The purpose of the conference was to assess the Holocaust as history or fiction, and whether the gas chambers were real. This, in spite of the fact that Holocaust denial is a crime in several European countries, including Germany.

Meanwhile, extremists make videos exhorting young girls as well as boys to kill Jews by becoming suicide bombers — in their view, martyrs. One girl who failed in a suicide mission was captured and is now in an Israeli prison. In an interview she proudly declared that she wanted to be the prettiest virgin in heaven. She doesn't realize that when you die, you're really dead.

I find all the hatred and violence sad because the Muslim world contains within itself the seeds of renewal. It cannot happen, though, as long as Jews and Americans are seen as the source of all that has gone wrong.

The Koran says, "Whoever slays a soul . . . it is as though he slew all men; and whoever keeps it alive, it is as though he kept alive all men."

I find it sad that with many people, Islam seems to have been twisted so that it limits what its adherents think. The Koran also says, "You shall have your religion and I shall have my religion."

I look at the older Kirk, so full of wisdom, yet so silent. "Hey, Silent Sam, what do you think? Do you know what I'm talking about? Aah, go back to sleep."

I walk away, musing over the answers as I bring my empty cup to the kitchen.

38
WRITING

I like to sit at the desk in my den, not so much to work as to look out the window at the rose garden that borders the house. Gazing back at me is the statue of the young nude lady that I brought over from Yugoslavia.

It is after the rain, and the roses have such wonderful colors. Mother Nature never makes a mistake. In the far corner is a huge bush of white roses all in bloom. The sky is stunning — fat, jolly cumulus clouds and in a large patch of blue sky rests a long cirrus cloud that looks like it came from a smokestack in heaven.

Turning away from this magical sight I spot, on the corner shelf, the books that I have written before this one. There are eight of them: three autobiographies, three novels, and two children's books. I can't believe that I've had the chutzpah to write eight books — me, an actor. Writing has taught me a lot about the world, but more about myself.

Everybody should write his or her autobiography. It doesn't have to be published; in writing it, you will get to know yourself. We are so busy living that we don't stop to take inventory. It's important to take inventory of your life to know what you have done that is good and what you have done that is bad. The way to grow in life is to know where you are and where you want to go. Writing an autobiography can make you a better person.

My Stroke of Luck brought me much gratification. I received many letters from stroke victims and from the relatives or friends of people who had experienced strokes. They were helped by my book and that pleased me very much.

One night I was surprised to receive a call from Luci Johnson, the daughter of President Johnson. She told me that she had bought my book and was reading it to her mother, Lady Bird. When I asked how her mother liked it, Luci replied, "She thinks it's great."

After we hung up, I inscribed a copy of my book to her:

Dear Lady Bird,
You are a big girl now. You should have your own book.

With much affection,
Kirk.

Some time ago, I visited several psychiatrists over a five-year period. I wanted to learn more about myself. All I learned is that everybody has problems and that my shrinks had more problems than I did.

Not surprisingly, my first book, *The Ragman's Son,* was especially important to me. It was the first time that I had written to learn about myself. My publisher was a little perturbed about the title.

"Why do you want to call it that?" he asked.

"Because that's what I am — a ragman's son — and I don't want to forget it."

I wrote it to find answers to questions like, Who am I? Where do I come from? And where am I going? I'm still asking those questions because I've changed over the years. We're changing all the time, so we have to keep asking ourselves these questions, as we all go in the same direction — the future.

39
TECHNOLOGY

I try to adhere to a work schedule. After my morning workout, I read, study, and take notes. The next day I take the notes to my office. Well, it's not really *my* office. The office belongs to Grace, my assistant. I inhabit a corner of her desk. When Grace knows I'm coming, she has ready for me a comfortable chair at the corner of her desk, a mug of cold water, and my glasses.

Grace is a very attractive African American woman who graduated from Dartmouth College and studied for a summer at the Yale School of Drama. When I asked her if she wanted to be an actress, she replied indignantly, "I *am* an actress. I just want a job."

I'm sure that before I finish this book she'll be working in the movies. Too bad, because she is a whiz at the computer.

I am in awe of technology. I ask, "Grace, did Martin Luther King ever talk about

Zionism?"

In a few minutes, the computer is buzzing and she prints out his words. I look at the computer. It is so thin. Does it really store all that information on a chip?

Really, I hate technology. I've never had a cell phone, although I insist that my wife carry one for protection. I never wear a wristwatch — I don't want to be reminded of the passage of time.

You walk along a street and many people you see are not there. Like zombies, they walk with cell phones pressed to their ears. In the cars that whiz by, many drivers are using cell phones. People riding bicycles are talking on cell phones! Mentally, they are somewhere else as they cause accidents.

Men, women, and children at home don't talk much with one another; they watch TV or use the computer. My grandchildren are guilty of this, too. Modern technology dominates their lives. I have often thought that technology is a curse.

That is, until technology saved my life. After months of physical therapy, my new knees were functioning perfectly. I was in tiptop shape. One day, though, I began to hemorrhage. I went to the doctor — my blood count was twenty-three. I didn't know what that meant, but the doctor said, "If my blood count was that low, I couldn't stand up."

He put me in the hospital, and they gave me a transfusion of four units of blood. My bleeding stopped — but why had it started? I then had an endoscopy to explore the upper region of my body. Next I had a colonoscopy to explore the lower region, and they still couldn't find the source of the bleeding.

"There is a new process that you could try," the doctor said. "You swallow a little camera while you wear a belt with a battery on one side and a recorder on the other."

I looked at him. "I swallow a camera?"

"Yes."

"Jeez, all my life I worked in front of the camera. I never swallowed one."

My joke fell flat. The doctor continued, "We take a constant video picture as the camera travels through your body. This is the only way we can see clearly a picture of the small intestine."

After fasting for a day, I swallowed the camera. It went down easily. For eight hours the camera recorded pictures of my insides. I couldn't believe that a camera had traveled through my whole body. As it did, it revealed where the bleeding was and how to stop it.

When the procedure was finished, they said I could go home.

"What about the camera?" I asked, pointing to my stomach.

The doctor laughed. "Oh, you can have it. When you eliminate it."

I searched, but I still haven't found it.

40
DOES GOD LAUGH?

Most people don't joke about the bible. As Walt Whitman wrote, "How many ages and generations have brooded and wept and agonized over this book!" But I find much humor in the Bible.

Once a week I study with Rabbi David Wolpe. I asked him, "Does God laugh?" and before he could answer I said, "I want to read you something. A friend of mine sent me this e-mail."

Noah's Ark Lesson 101 — Everything you need to know you can learn from Noah's Ark:

1. Don't miss the boat.
2. Remember that we are all in the same boat.
3. Plan ahead. It wasn't raining when Noah built the Ark.
4. Stay fit. When you're 600 years old,

someone may ask you to do something really big.
5. Don't listen to critics; just get on with the job that needs to be done.
6. Build your future on high ground.
7. For safety's sake, travel in pairs.
8. Speed isn't always an advantage. The snails were on board with the cheetahs.
9. When you're stressed, float awhile.
10. Remember, the Ark was built by amateurs, the *Titanic* by professionals.

The rabbi looked at me with a smile. "If God read that, I think He would laugh."

"But can God read?" I asked.

The rabbi glanced at his watch. "Your time is up, we'll discuss that next week."

My Hebrew is limited so I study the Torah in an English translation. Studying doesn't make me more Jewish, but it does make me more understanding. The Torah acknowledges that people aren't perfect. We have sinned, but we can make amends, ask for forgiveness, forgive others who have hurt us, and become better people.

■ ■ ■ ■

Yom Kippur, the Day of Atonement, is a frightening day for me. Jews pray, "Who among us is righteous enough to say, 'I have not sinned'?" We say, "We confess, we have gone astray, we have sinned, we have trespassed." This sermon builds to a chilling climax with a blowing of the shofar, a ram's horn. You begin to believe that the wail of the shofar is heard by God. You cannot be indifferent.

Some things in the Bible make me laugh. They say Jews are smart, but in the Book of Judges, you'll find one of the dumbest Jews who ever lived. Samson, the strongest man in the world, hooked up with the sexy Delilah of the Philistines, enemies of the Israelites. She wheedled out of him the secret of his strength — it was his hair.

So the Philistines cut off his hair while he slept and put the weakened Samson in a dungeon. But they proved to be even dumber than Samson — they never gave him another haircut. His hair grew and so did his strength. He used it to knock down the pillars of the temple and kill all the people inside.

Of course, it's hard for me to believe that

this really happened, but it makes a good story and dramatic material for a movie.

Why was God so talkative thousands of years ago? Was He really talking? God said so many things thousands of years ago. Why is He silent now? Can it be that we are not on the right frequency?

Maybe He was a godly inspiration within man. I am bothered by all the magic: a burning bush that never consumed itself, Jesus walking on water, water changed into wine.

I am a Jew but that doesn't mean I think that all the many stories in the Bible are true. They may be just metaphors. But I like those stories. They have proved to me that throughout history man has needed to believe in a higher power — some of these he created by his own hand, as with idols, and some he created with his own spirit.

I believe in a higher power. You can call Him Allah, Adonai, God, the Buddha, or the Intelligent Creator. I don't know if we are created in God's image, but I would hate to think of a God with genitals. Maybe He's a ray of light? It doesn't matter. I recognize a higher power and I pray to Him.

I am deeply moved by a powerful statement made by a rabbi, Hillel, who lived in the first century B.C. He was asked by a student, "Rabbi, can you tell me the essence of Judaism standing on one foot?"

The rabbi looked straight into the eyes of the student and said, "Don't do to others what you would not like done to you. The rest is commentary."

The rabbi doesn't ask you to be guided literally by the stories in the Bible — he refers to them as commentary. The goal of religions should be to make better people who care for others. So whatever works for you, fine. If everyone adhered to Hillel's statement, though, our grandchildren would be better people and would live in a peaceful world. That works for me.

I look out the window. It's dark, and I can barely make out the silhouette of my nude statue. I am tired. Lying at my feet, Danny and Foxy look tired, too. They follow me into the kitchen — they know what comes next. Their tails wag as they hear the crinkling sound when I take two cookies out of the bag. I open the door, give them each a treat, and they go happily to their kennel. I go to bed.

41
GREED IS NOT GOOD

When an actor makes it in Hollywood, he earns more money than he can imagine, and he is often dumbfounded. What to do with it all? Years ago, people advised me to have a business manager. Coincidentally, a lawyer who worked at my agency, Famous Artists, was leaving to become a business manager. I relaxed — I would have a friend handling my affairs. Things went well; I made lots of money. Sam, my new business manager, gave me financial reports that I didn't understand and papers to sign. I signed away everything until I was broke. My wife discovered the ruse.

Different versions of this story can be told and retold by many actors in the cinema world. Of course, most of us are ashamed to tell it. Nobody wants to look like an idiot. I didn't. Yet I often sing to my children, "Don't worry about strangers. Keep your eye on your best friend."

What happens privately on a relatively small scale is mirrored by what goes on publicly within big corporations. The world was shocked to see so many heads of our biggest corporations become infected with greed. Even though they had so much money, they still wanted more. They raised their salaries and their pensions; they cooked the books and stole money from their shareholders and their employees. I think greed becomes a disease, and it's sometimes incurable.

My son Michael is partly responsible for the cultural acceptance of greed. In 1987 he made a movie, *Wall Street,* about corporate skullduggery for which he got his second Oscar. In one scene Michael as Gordon Gekko, speaking to his board, says:

The point is, ladies and gentlemen, that greed, for lack of a better word, is good. Greed is right. Greed works. Greed clarifies, cuts through and captures the essence of the evolutionary spirit. Greed, in all its forms — greed for life, for money, for love, knowledge — has marked the upward surge of mankind.

Michael was just too good an actor. Gordon Gekko was a fictional character modeled on the corporate raider Ivan Boesky; today he would have been modeled on Kenneth Lay, John Rigas, Sam Waksal, Bernard Ebbers, or Dennis Kozlowski. For these CEOs, there were no limits.

How can we hope to spread democracy around the world when there is so much corruption in our own country? Our democracy is based on capitalism. When capitalism falters, the underpinnings of democracy are weakened. The corruption within our big corporations has hurt global democracy. We must clean up our act first before we dare to ask the world to follow our lead.

We are trying to spread democracy in Iraq. Meanwhile, the American companies rebuilding the country are filled with corruption. The Iraqis know it.

How can we tell Muslim countries, which resent our interference, to clean up their act? How can we tell the king of Saudi Arabia to tone it down? The king built himself a vacation retreat in Marbella, Spain, complete with a modern telecommunications center to cater to his majesty's business needs and a fully equipped hospital to protect his majesty's health. There are also three Boeing airplanes, several helicopters, four yachts, and hundreds of cars (Mercedeses and Rolls-Royces) ready to whisk the king and his entourage wherever he might want to go.

Here is the punch line: the king's retreat looks out on a beautiful beach for nudists. At home, the king's women are covered from head to toe. According to *Paris Match,* in the last thirty years, the king has visited this oasis only four times. But for that millions and millions have been spent. Where do kings and dictators get the money to live in splendor while their people often live in poverty? In this case, oil. Bin Laden, the son of a billionaire, attacked the corruption of the Saudi Arabian monarchy before he started his program of terror.

Not every CEO is a crook. Bill Gates, probably the richest man in the world, announced that he would withdraw from running his corporation, Microsoft. He wants to devote all of his energy to philanthropic efforts and concentrate on world health and education as he travels around Africa with his wife, Melinda. Mr. and Mrs. Gates are giving more than $6 billion to global health. Melinda said, "We're not anxious to leave a lot of money to our children."

Warren Buffett, another billionaire, was very impressed with the work that Bill Gates and his wife are doing. He decided to contribute $30 billion to the Gates Foundation, which is now worth more than $60 billion. Together they will work to find cures for diseases that afflict the world's children.

This team serves as a model for all CEOs. Bill Gates said, "Our schools are obsolete," and he is right. Because students are too young to vote we neglect them. We must improve our schools and acquire better equipment, computers, enough skilled teachers, and much more. This takes money, but the budget for education in this country is always shortchanged.

In Kirk Douglas High School we're installing a new system of computers. My son Peter, who is president of my foundation, is in charge. He's a whiz at computers and I'm a dummy. Through our foundation he's making a deal to computerize the school. It will have the best computer system of any school in L.A. That's a small step in the right direction.

In this crazy world we must be concerned with what will happen to our children and grandchildren. They are our greatest resource. Now, they are dozing in baby carriages, sliding down slides, and studying in schools. We need to prepare them to face their future lives.

Are we doing a good job? No. Students drop out at an alarming rate before they graduate from high school. None of our teachers is paid adequately. We have to make sure that all of our young citizens have what I had after my parents came here from Russia — a chance to do something with their lives. We must give our future citizens the chances that we had and more.

42
STONES AND FLOWERS

I like Munich; it's a wonderful city. In 1957 we shot *Paths of Glory* in Germany. I learned to speak German. I tried to forget that Hitler rose to power there, but anti-Semitism started long before that in Germany.

As the Catholic church spread in Western Europe, Jews were among the only people who resisted changing their religion. Anti-Semitism was rampant in Germany, and although rich Jews were tolerated, poor Jews were treated like animals. At the border, they were taxed like merchandise. There were strict regulations to keep all Jews lacking visible means of support out of Berlin. The only professional field open to Jews was medicine. I don't know why.

Despite the prejudice, Jews began to live in symbiosis with the Germans. Many impoverished aristocrats sought to marry the daughters of wealthy Jewish parents. There was a wave of conversions — the poet

Heinrich Heine, Karl Marx, and others. I don't know how many were sincere.

Rich Jewish women held salons for both Jews and gentiles in their houses, although Jews were rarely invited to German homes. Many Germans were delighted to come and share ideas with the Jewish intelligentsia. Young Jews volunteered for army service. They began to feel that they belonged, which was rare for Jews. It was "a heavenly feeling to possess a fatherland," Amos Elon wrote in *The Pity of It All*.

And then Hitler arrived.

I consider the Olympic Games very important. They unite the countries of the world in friendly competition. I worked for the Olympic Committee in the United States, and in 1972 my wife and I went to Munich for the Olympics. We watched the parade of athletes marching into the stadium, including the tiny contingent of Israelis who would soon be kidnapped by terrorists.

I can still see that terrorist in a ski mask standing proudly on the balcony of the Israeli athletes' quarters. A group of terrorists climbed over the fence and entered the Israeli compound. Where were the German security guards?

We saw Mark Spitz win his seventh gold

medal in swimming. Then we had to leave Munich. The airport was closed, though, because the Israeli athletes were being held prisoner by terrorists at the airport. The Israelis requested permission to send their own terror squad to help, but permission was denied.

Because Mark Spitz was a Jew, he was quickly rushed out of the country. The public followed this drama, glued to the TV. As we all know, eleven young Israeli athletes were murdered.

Then another drama ensued. A memorial service was conducted the next day, but the names of the murdered athletes were not even mentioned. Avery Brundage, the head of the U.S. Olympic Committee, felt that the "incident" should not mar the Olympics and the games continued. Jim Murray, a *Los Angeles Times* columnist, said, "Incredibly, they're going on with it. It's almost like having a dance at Dachau."

In 1936 Avery Brundage had sent an American team to Hitler's games in Berlin and replaced the only two Jews on the team with non-Jewish athletes (luckily, one of them was Jesse Owens, a black athlete). In 1941, because of his Nazi allegiance, Brundage was expelled from the antiwar America First Committee.

The film *Munich* was made to honor the Israeli Olympians who were murdered. It received some very positive reviews at the beginning of 2006, but many critics destroyed it. Some blamed the Jewish screenwriter, Tony Kushner, but Steven Spielberg was the boss and cowriter.

In one scene, the Israeli government is portrayed as being very concerned about the money spent on the Olympic venture. "We need receipts," one character says. "We're not Rothschilds." That made some people wince, but I interpreted it to mean that Israel is a small country with a limited budget. It had to be very careful how it spent money, even in tracking down terrorists.

I thought that Steven went too far in his attempt to show so eloquently the Palestinian side at the expense of the Israeli point of view, but I don't agree with the severity of the negative criticism. To me, the film explored how emotionally difficult it is for Israelis to hunt and kill terrorists.

In one scene the Israelis are very concerned that they kill the terrorists without hurting a child. At the same time, of course, they could not capture the terrorists and try them, as they did Adolf Eichmann.

The last scene showed a sabra, a born Israeli, who could not deal with the killing. That is probably the reaction of many Israelis.

At the same time, Israel is dedicated to fighting for its independence — its very survival — and it has concluded that it must fight back against any attack.

Steven Spielberg established an organization named Shoah (Hebrew for Holocaust) that interviewed all the remaining Jews who had survived the Holocaust that he could find. This was a very difficult undertaking because old age was diminishing the number of survivors. I went to his studio to see what he had done. It was so touching, almost unbearable. These elderly survivors — men and women, each with a tattooed number on his or her arm — talked about their experiences. Their stories were so different and yet all the same. Some people spoke with laughter, some with bitterness, others in apathetic monotones. It was painful to sit through it.

Steven also made *Schindler's List*, about a Nazi womanizer and alcoholic who helped the Jews. In the final scene in the movie, survivors and their children file by the grave of Oskar Schindler in Jerusalem. In accordance with Jewish custom and with solemn ceremony, each places a small stone on the grave to indicate that a visit of respect has been paid. (On my last visit there I did as well.)

I asked Rabbi Wolpe, with whom I study the Talmud, "Why leave stones rather than flowers?"

"The prevailing Jewish view," he answered, "was that bringing flowers smacks of a pagan custom. That is why today one rarely sees flowers on the graves in traditional Jewish cemeteries. Instead there are stones, small and large, piled without pattern on the grave. For most of us, stones conjure a harsh image. It does not seem the appropriate memorial for one who has died. But stones have a special character in Judaism. The stone upon which Abraham takes his son to be sacrificed is called the foundation stone of the world. The most sacred shrine in Judaism, after all, is a pile of stones — the wall of the Second Temple."

Flowers are a good metaphor for life. Life withers; it fades like a flower. As Isaiah says, "All flesh is grass, and all its beauty like the flowers of the field; grass withers and flowers fade."

While flowers may be a good metaphor for the brevity of life, stones seem better suited to the permanence of memory. Stones do not die.

When we place stones on a grave and inscribe a motto above the stone, we are asking God to keep the departed's soul in His sling. Among all the souls whom God has to watch over, we wish to add the name — the pebble — of the soul of our departed.

There is something that suits the antiquity and solidity of Judaism in the symbolism of a stone. In moments when we face the fragility of life, Judaism reminds us that there is permanence amid the pain. While other things fade, stones and souls endure.

As I've said, each week my wife and I visit the grave of our beloved son Eric. Anne brings flowers. I bring a small stone.

43
AM I A GOOD FATHER?

June 2006 was graduation day at Kirk Douglas High School. When I arrived at the school, the mural on the wall was still there, along with the camera, my name, and the rolls of film. Students had begun to paint the titles of some of my pictures on the strips of film. I was impressed.

When I entered the crowded auditorium I was greeted with the same rock band I'd heard before, playing a new song they had composed. A girl sang, "Thank you, Mr. D." It was a happy song and she sang it well.

I gave a short talk to the graduating class. I talked about the death of my son Eric from drugs. I don't know if the kids ever discuss drugs with their parents, but they seemed to listen attentively.

Then came the happy part of the tribute: the five-hundred-dollar checks to the graduates. I said, "When I first started there were only three graduates. Now there are twenty.

Are you guys trying to break me?"

We left on a happy note.

Not long ago, Michael and I made a documentary, *A Father . . . A Son . . . Once upon a Time in Hollywood,* and the rest of the family chimed in. It was not a commercial enterprise; we both chipped in for the production costs. We thought it would be good for our children and grandchildren to have a film that didn't feature actors playing parts but us being ourselves. The documentary dealt with the relationship between the ragman's son and the star's son. I decided that life was more difficult for the son of a star than for the son of a ragman.

We didn't follow any scripts — it was spontaneous. That can be dangerous.

When I heard my wife talking about an affair I had had years ago, I was shocked. When I heard my son Joel say, "Living with dad was like living in a beautiful town next to a volcano," I was shocked again. Could they be talking about me?

I thought of a line in the Scottish poem by Robert Burns, "O wad some Power the giftie gie us, To see oursels as ithers see us!" Yes, it's difficult to see ourselves as others see us.

In a scene where Michael and I were sitting at the table, talking, I asked, "Michael, was I a good father?"

Michael looked at me and paused — it was a very long pause.

Finally, he answered quietly, "Ultimately, you were a great father."

I studied him. He seemed to be serious.

"Ultimately?" I asked.

He nodded his head. "Yes."

That scene haunted me. The compliment he paid me became smaller and smaller, but the pause . . . became bigger and bigger. Ultimately? I began to fill in the pause. When his mother and I divorced, amicably, Michael was about eight. I stayed in California working in movies. Diana, Michael, and Joel moved to New York. When I visited them for the first time, I kissed Diana on the cheek. Michael burst out crying.

"Why are you crying?" I asked.

Through his tears, he said, "I thought you were mad at Mommy."

It's difficult to know how a divorce hurts children. When I was making *Act of Love* in Paris I arranged for my sons Michael and Joel to visit me, and I suggested that their mother come, too, instead of a nanny. One day we all took a walk in the Bois de Boulogne. I was holding Michael's hand. He suddenly took my other hand and put it in Diana's hand, saying, "Now the family is together." Diana and I looked at each other but said nothing.

A few days later Diana and the children went back to New York and I returned to L.A. Of course, I kept in contact with my family, but I was doing film after film and woman after woman. I didn't have much time. Fortunately, Diana eventually married a great guy, Bill Darrid. He was a wonderful surrogate father, but he wasn't Michael's father, and he died at an early age.

I began to fill in that long pause. I became a great father when I needed my sons more than they needed me.

After Eric's death, I needed him so much. He was the only son I had ever spanked. I tried to push away that memory and another popped up: that of Pa standing in front of our dilapidated house as my mother and sisters and I were moving. He stared at me but didn't speak.

Why am I leaving my father? I asked myself. I kept staring at him. He said nothing and went into the house.

Did Michael and Joel feel that I had walked away, too?

Did Eric feel that I had walked away?

I felt guilty the day I sat at the gravesite and spoke to him.

"You know, Eric, years ago when Louis Jourdan's boy died your mother and I were very sad. It must be terrible to lose a son, we thought. When Ray Stark's son committed suicide we thought the same thing. Little did we know that we would lose you in the future. I'm sure that when anyone loses a child they feel a sense of guilt. What did I do wrong? I have wrestled with that for some time. I always remind myself of how often we tried to help you — the visits we made to the various rehabilitation centers that tried to get you well. I never asked any of my sons to become Jewish and have a bar mitzvah. It was a surprise to me when you wrote that you were studying to become bar mitzvahed. One Saturday you went through the service and became a Jew. I was not there, and that haunts me, that was a secret that I hid somewhere deep inside of me. Maybe you did it to reach out for me and I was not there. I'm sorry that I didn't come."

Forgive me.

44
DON'T BE TOO
RELIGIOUS

Religion endangered my life when I was a boy. Coming home from Hebrew school every day I had to pass the Lark Street Gang. They waited for me holding women's stockings packed with pebbles.

"Here he comes!" they shouted as they went after me swinging their weapons. "Kike, Jew bastard, Christ killer!"

I just kept running as fast as I could, and I survived.

Religion has killed many people. The Inquisition murdered Jews and Muslims. Before Constantine embraced Catholicism, Christians were crucified by the Romans. The Crusaders murdered all non-Christians, Jews and Muslims alike, in their path to the holy city, Jerusalem. In early history, Jews and Muslims were persecuted equally.

I'm an American Jew, a secular Jew, and I go to temple only on the High Holidays. I am intrigued by Ecclesiastes 4:17: "Be not overeager to go to the house of God." Just going to church does not make you a good person. You go to church and praise God for all the things He knows. Yes, He is omniscient, ubiquitous, and omnipotent, but what about you? Are you a worthy person? Your actions in life decide what you are. Are you honest? Are you charitable? Do you help others? Or do you use regular attendance every Friday or Saturday or Sunday to salve your conscience about other activities? Don't be too religious — it's dangerous.

Now, we have almost reached the Apocalypse. Many Islamist Muslims are ready to kill anyone who doesn't believe in Allah. It is hard to accept their interpretation of the holy Koran, which they believe tells them to kill all "infidels."

Some Christians and Jews have tried to understand each other's worth. Sister Rose Thering was a Catholic nun who dedicated her life to bridging the gap between Christianity and Judaism. Unsettled by the horrors of the Holocaust, she began to examine what the church taught children about the Jews.

"When I began to read the textbooks,"

she said, "it almost made me ill."

She spent her life promoting greater understanding between Christians and Jews. She wore a Star of David fused to the cross on her neck, and she closed her letters with the Hebrew word shalom — peace.

Reverend Steven Swope, the minister of a Christian congregation, has found another solution. "Jesus is *our* way but other people have other ways." He has arranged for Muslims to place prayer rugs on the floor and worship Allah on Friday, for Jews to use the church on Saturday, and of course Christians use it on Sunday.

David Gridin, the president of a Hebrew college, and Dr. Peterson, the head of a Christian theological seminary, have also found a solution: they, too, share the same space. They believe it's a wonderful thing for Jews and Christians to study together. It has forged a deeper connection with their own faiths. They encourage college students to attend one another's services and classes.

There are not many places where Christian and Jewish congregations share the same space. This is a wonderful way for different religions to function in harmony. Think of the money they will save by using one plot of land and one building. I suspect it will never catch on — it's too good to be true — but I applaud their efforts.

Recently, Mr. Ghali, a Palestinian refugee from Lebanon, wanted to build a new mosque in San Francisco. He admitted that he had been raised since childhood to hate Shiites, Christians, and especially Jews. He found a perfect place to open a mosque. The Jewish owner wanted to charge more than the group could afford, though — ten thousand dollars a month. Mr. Ghali was dumbfounded when the landlord then said, "A mosque? Fantastic. We have so many fanatics. We need to work together for peace." He gave the mosque a long-term lease and cut the rent by 80 percent. Mr. Ghali was ecstatic and started a movement to shape an "American Muslim identity" with tolerance and respect for other faiths, including Jews. His dreams were shattered by an Egyptian imam, Safwat Morsy, who opened a new mosque just around the corner. Crowds came and Sheik Safwat preached for a jihad, a holy war, against Israel and against United States forces in Iraq and Afghanistan.

How sad that the efforts of Mr. Ghali to present the peaceful side of Islam — founded on compassion, respect, dignity, and love — failed. The fight continues. How will it end?

There is a section in Brooklyn, New York, that has become a self-imposed ghetto of Ultra-Orthodox Hasidic Jews. The men wear black suits, matching black hats, and beards. The women wear long dresses and stay subservient. They keep to themselves and don't welcome intruders. I can't help but admire how they adhere to customs that began more than a thousand years ago, but I also think they must join modern society.

In another part of the world monks live an isolated life on a mountaintop and spend their days praying to God.

It might be easy to be holy while alone on a mountaintop, but it's better to try to be holy down below with the people.

I believe God, however you perceive Him, wants you to participate in the world. He wants you to enjoy the beauty of the world and face its challenges. He wants you to help one another. He wants different people to do different things; maybe everyone has his or her own special mission.

Robert Browning wrote, "A man's reach should far exceed his grasp, else what's a heaven for?"

Somewhere each day — in bed, in my car, walking down a crowded street — I murmur this prayer that I learned from a Hebrew prayer book:

Oh God, how can we know You? Where can we find You? You are as close to us as breathing, yet You are farther than the farthermost star. You are as mysterious as the vast solitude of night, yet as familiar to us as the light of the sun. Where can we find You?

Keep seeking God. If you don't find Him, He will find you.

45

HOLD THE
GEFILTE FISH

It's been a tough day. I go to bed and turn
on the television. David Letterman is on
and my son Michael is his guest. They are
talking about his golf tournament, which is
called Michael Douglas and Friends.

"Will your father be in attendance?"

"No," answers Michael.

"Doesn't he play golf?"

"He started me on the game."

"How did that go?"

Michael begins to laugh. David asks,
"What's so funny?"

"Well, my father was giving me some
pointers about driving. He said put your
body behind the swing. I swung at the ball
as hard as I could." Michael begins to laugh
again.

"Come on, tell me what's so funny."

"Well, I hit the ball with the back of the
club and it spurted out and hit my father
right in the crotch."

I can feel the pain now and I turn off the television. I pick up the *New York Times* that I didn't have time to read this morning. Always bad news. I turn over a page.

What's this? A talking fish! In New Square Fish Market, there was a miracle. A twenty-pound carp was about to be slaughtered into gefilte fish. The cutter was about to club it in the head with a rubber hammer when the fish began speaking in Hebrew.

The fish cutter, Luis Nivelo, was not a Jew and didn't understand what the fish was saying. He called his boss, Mr. Rosen, a Hasidic Jew with eleven children. Rosen understood. The flopping fish was crying out, "Tzaruch shemirah hasof bah," which means, "Account for yourself, the end is near." In a panic, Mr. Rosen tried to kill the carp with a machete. The fish bucked and Mr. Rosen cut off his own thumb. He was rushed to the hospital.

As for the talking carp, it was chopped into gefilte fish. For the fish, the end really was near.

Some Hasidic sects believe that people can be reincarnated as fish. Why not?

I lie there in the dark. The quiet of the house is interrupted only by Danny and Foxy barking at a neighbor's cat.

312

I keep thinking of that talking carp. In ancient days, God spoke a lot from a burning bush. I haven't heard of Him speaking for many years. Why not?

I fall asleep. Suddenly I sense an intense light over my head. I try to open my eyes but the light is too bright. "Oh my God," I whisper.

"Yeesss."

A voice? Far away — yet very near. Could it be a carp?

"Issur."

He addresses me by my given name! He can't be a fish.

"Issur," He says in a louder voice.

Oh my God . . . it's GOD! "How are things with you?" I wince. Here I am talking to God, and the best I can do is make small talk.

But He answers, "I have been scrutinizing My universe." His voice sounds like that of James Earl Jones. "My eyes drifted across the Milky Way and stopped at a planet — the one you call Mars. I don't like that name, too warlike." He hesitates. I wonder what He is getting at. "Mars, as you call it, was once a flourishing sphere — much like your own planet earth. I gave them free will, too. They continually abused it." There is anger in His voice. "Now the planet is barren, arid, and forlorn."

I try to peek again but the light is still too bright. Nobody will believe me. I lie there quietly.

"Millions of years later, I decided to try again." His voice is now tempered by sadness. "Another planet with life. If at first you don't succeed, try again, I always say."

"I always say that, too," I respond, trying to build a little common ground.

"Yes," He whispers, "I know. What a disappointment!" What does He mean? "Ever since Cain killed his brother Abel, people are murdering one another." His voice keeps rising. "Nations use their finest brains to create bombs so devastating they could destroy all I have created. Airplanes are flown into buildings, killing thousands of innocent men, women, and children. In other parts of the world, millions upon millions of children starve to death. Young people blow themselves up and expect to get seventy-two virgins in heaven. Do you think I run a brothel here? Choose life!"

A long silence. Maybe, I think, I can cheer Him up a little. "Lord, I know awful things have happened all over the world, but aren't you proud of our country? We put a man on the moon!"

"Keep off my property!" He shouts. I pull

the covers over my head. "You have spent billions and billions of dollars, why?" He didn't wait for an answer. "*Ego!* The Soviets were the first to put a man in space. So now you spend billions to reach other planets. Why? People are starving, dying of AIDS. Children need schools. That money could be spent to help people, not to see how far you can go in My universe." His voice is dripping with sarcasm.

There is a long pause but I don't dare say anything. I want to ask, just to clarify, if He really is the same God the Muslims pray to — I know my rabbi will be very interested — but before I can figure out how to phrase the question, He says suddenly, in a flat tone, "I'm considering changing this planet to match Mars."

I hold my breath, shaking under the blanket.

He is still angry. "I had such high hopes for this country. Democracy! Free will! All people created equal. They thrive! Gain wealth and power. I prayed they would be an example to the rest of the world."

I wonder who He prays to. I try to open my eyes to see Him but the light is still too bright. Now His tone is almost a whisper. Through the covers I strain to hear Him.

"Do you know the words on the Statue of

Liberty?" He asks.

"Yes." This will impress him. I throw the covers off. "Give me your tired, your poor —"

He cuts me off. "*Enough!* Do you think you're auditioning for something?"

I pull the covers over myself. "And don't be so smug," He continues. "Countries look up to America and what do they see? A church established in My name that harbors pedophiles. I weep for the victims scarred for life." I slink under the covers thinking, well, it's not *my* church.

"That's exactly the problem!"

Oh my God, He's reading my mind.

His voice grows louder. "You're all just thinking about yourselves! If you don't take responsibility for your world — all of it — and try to do something, you will wind up a burnt-out cinder." He accentuates each syllable. I hold my breath. Then He continues. "When I gave you free will I wanted to bring love, not hate."

I poke my head out from under the blankets, my eyes still shut. "I will tell them how You feel," I say quickly.

He laughs harshly, and I cover up again.

"Will anybody believe that you talked with Me?" He asks.

I lie still in my bed, scarcely breathing. I

picture a vast rugged terrain, barren, arid, and so silent.

I wait, but He says nothing more. The bright light disappears and I blink my eyes open in the dark. A wind ruffles the curtain. I rush to the window and look out at the pitch-black night. A sudden blast of lightning brightens the world. For a second, I can clearly see all the trees and houses around me. Then again pure darkness, and silence, broken by a far-off roll of thunder.

I'm suddenly awakened by Lettie with my coffee and newspaper.

"Hold the gefilte fish," I blurt out.

46

WHO'S MINDING THE STORE?

What a stupid thing to say! I rub my aching head, still haunted by the nightmare. I may not be getting any smarter as I get older, but I'm much more concerned about life around me. Life seems more precious than it ever has — maybe because I've used up most of mine or because I want my grandchildren's lives to be as good as possible.

Our planet is like a vast community of homes that we have rented. When we leave them for the next occupant they should be neat and clean. But let's face it, all the homes on the planet are in a mess and nobody seems to care enough to do what is necessary to fix them. Perhaps if our politicians were allowed to pass only laws that benefited their grandchildren, we'd be in better shape. Somehow, our leaders seem to have disappeared and our priorities have been turned upside down. If my company, Bryna, were being run as our country is, I would fire the leaders of Bryna — my wife and myself. We are in charge of its artistic and financial ventures, so the buck stops here.

I look around and everywhere I see things going badly. The tragedy of 9/11 should have been a wake-up call. We saw pictures on TV that looked like the end of the world — billowing smoke rising from two of our tallest buildings, hundred-story buildings falling to the ground, people jumping to their deaths, three thousand fatalities. We believed that we were impenetrable — wars were fought far away from our shores — but we were attacked and it shocked everyone. What may be even worse is that our government ignored the hints and indications that something major was about to happen. The CIA didn't communicate with the FBI; valuable information didn't get to the top.

Who was minding the store?

Amidst the smoldering debris of the World Trade Center our president shouted through a bullhorn to the world that we will "find those responsible and bring them to justice." Yet instead he declared war on Iraq, and Osama bin Laden escaped capture. We didn't send enough troops and we wound up with a civil war and hundreds of people dying every day. Was that the best use of our people and our money?

Then came Hurricane Katrina, swirling into the Gulf of Mexico en route to our southern shores. Authorities had known for years that the levees of New Orleans were vulnerable but they never did anything about it. And when the inevitable disaster struck, the delayed reaction to it compounded the destruction. FEMA, managed by the president's incompetent cronies, took days to come to the rescue of people who were drowning in flooded homes. The citizens, mostly African Americans, were squeezed into the filthy Superdome for four days before buses arrived to take them out of the city. As water was pumped out of the streets into Lake Pontchartrain, the mayor gave people the order to come back to the city just when tropical storm Rita was bearing down on them. On the highway, policemen yelled to the snarl of city-bound traffic, "Go back, go back!" Who was minding the store?

In Lebanon, when the war started between Hezbollah and Israel, thousands of tourists were caught in the country. France and Italy immediately sent ships to rescue their citizens, but our U.S. citizens were stuck in

Lebanon for days with missiles flying overhead.

What were our priorities?

I take a big swallow of coffee and pick up the newspaper. The headline hits me: "NASA Slams a Space Probe into a Comet." I shudder. Does NASA know what it's doing? The aim was to unlock secrets of the origins of the solar system. I could hear His voice shouting, *"Keep off my property!"* I shudder again. Our country should look into the problems of our own planet rather than spending billions of dollars looking into space. We've known for years that the planet is warmer than it has been, but nobody in the U.S. government does anything serious to avert this catastrophe in the making.

The space program started because of ego. Russia was the first country to send two men into space. Challenged into competing with our Cold War adversary, President Kennedy then vowed to send a man to the moon. Maybe if China decides to lead the world in cleaning up its environment, the United States will finally be goaded into doing something about global warming.

I once invited the Russian cosmonauts Georgi Beregovoy and Konstantin Feoktistov to a cocktail party at my house along with the most beautiful starlets in Hollywood. My Russian friends were impressed. Through an interpreter, Beregovoy pointed out to me the actress he wanted to take into outer space.

I remember being invited to the Johnson Space Center in Houston, Texas. I was allowed to go into a simulator and practice lining up my capsule with another capsule in outer space. It was exciting. I actually felt as if I was far above our planet earth — but I was unable to join up the capsules. It's a good thing they wouldn't let me be an astronaut.

In 1971 Henry Kissinger invited my family to Cape Kennedy to witness the launch of *Apollo 14.* My main recollection was fright. When the rocket ignited, the earth trembled as if an earthquake had struck, rocking and rolling to an ear-piercing wail. When *Apollo 14* was out of sight, Anne took Peter and Eric back to Miami to catch a flight to California. I flew to New York with Henry Kissinger on a private plane. I sat discreetly in the back of the plane while, up front, Henry and an Austrian ambassador carried on a conversation in German. It all felt civilized.

Since then, things haven't gone so well.

NASA has spent millions and millions of dollars trying to deal with the foam that caused the destruction of the *Columbia* space shuttle, killing seven astronauts. So far, space exploration has resulted in the deaths of eighteen astronauts in flight accidents and seventy ground crew members in launchpad accidents. At one time, we needed the manned space program so that we could feel proud of our country. Do we still need it?

What should our priorities be?

The Mars rovers *Spirit* and *Opportunity* have done a fine job. They have traveled hundreds of millions of miles without humans. They carry the most sophisticated instruments and have sent back detailed images of panoramic views of Mars and other far-off planets such as Jupiter. NASA expected the rovers to last for about ninety days in the harsh landscape of Mars. Instead, they exceeded all expectations and are still sending data and pictures home.

In space travel, robots do a better job than humans do. They are much cheaper to send into space and to maintain — they don't eat or drink. Why not continue with that miniaturization program and eliminate the high cost of sending people into space, risking their lives in the process? This would cut billions of dollars from the budget each year.

We are spending billions if not trillions of dollars in Iraq. Our efforts to clean up the mess in New Orleans were handled poorly and at great cost. Our debt is soaring into the trillions. Who is going to pay for this, our grandchildren? We need to clarify our priorities. We can always go back to sending a man into space when we can afford it.

We are the strongest country in the world. We are the only superpower, but the United States is operating like a huge Rube Goldberg machine with no one in charge of it. Bureaucrats fall over each other every time there is an emergency. Thousands of lives are lost because we know too little too late. We idly stand by and shake our heads with regret and blame each time a new catastrophe occurs. I can hear God's voice ringing in my ear.

We must leave our homes — our planet — in good order for our grandchildren to inherit. We cannot leave a legacy of incompetence. We made the mess, we must clean it up.

Let's face it — no one wants to move into a dirty house.

I am anxious to go back to bed. Maybe He has something more to say.

47
ISRAEL

Sitting in the garden across the pool from my dual bust, my table littered with paper, I am looking again at a transcript of an interview that former president Jimmy Carter gave to the German magazine *Der Spiegel* in August 2006. Carter's face glares at me from the cover of his November 2006 book, *Palestine: Peace Not Apartheid.* Several articles that were e-mailed to me criticizing his book are also on the table. Looking at the mess makes me angry. I shout across the pool at myself, "It's time to get rid of you guys — they're out to get you!" I suddenly see Lettie heading to the alley with a bag of trash. She looks bewildered — she must have heard me.

I say calmly, "Is my wife home yet?"

"No, Mr. Douglas, she's still at the office," she says, hurrying to the alley.

Lettie must think I am crazy. She is used to me talking to myself, but now I am yelling. I pick up the transcript of President Carter's interview. I can't believe that he feels our attempts to spread democracy in the Middle East were dented by "the United States supporting and encouraging Israel in this unjustified attack on Lebanon," referring to Israel's 2006 invasion of southern Lebanon in retaliation for Hezbollah rocket attacks in northern Israel. The reporter from *Der Spiegel* argued, "But wasn't Israel the first to get attacked?" Think of it, a German reporter contradicting President Carter's criticism of our ally Israel. Carter answered, "I don't think that Israel has any legal or moral justification for their massive bombing of the entire nation of Lebanon."

When I read the article, I was very upset and I sent him a letter:

Dear Mr. President,
With all the warm feelings that I have for you and Rosalynn, I never thought that you would make me cry. I was dumbfounded by your negative remarks about Israel in your interview with *Der Spiegel.* Israel did not start the war. Hezbollah rained bombs on Israel indiscriminately, two soldiers were kidnapped, and eight were killed. Those bombs never stopped.

Of course, I sympathize with the Lebanese civilians who have been killed in the bombing. The Israeli bombs were always aimed at the section in Lebanon used as a base by Hezbollah. Israeli planes showered Lebanon with pamphlets warning the civilians when they would strike. In contrast, Hezbollah fired over a hundred bombs every day with no regard to where they fell. Lebanon allowed Hezbollah to prepare the southern part of Lebanon for war over a six-year period.

Israel has had to endure many wars against overwhelming odds. If Israel loses one war, they lose Israel. The saying goes: "If the Arabs put down their weapons today, there would be no more violence. But if the Jews put down their weapons today, there would be no more Israel."

Israel is the only successful democracy in the Mideast. Israel is our ally; they proved that during the Cold War with Russia. Every attempt to give up land for peace — in Gaza and the West Bank — has been interpreted as weakness on the part of Israel. My heart goes out to all people who suffer because of war, the thousands of our soldiers in Iraq, and the many Israelis who have been killed by suicide bombers in pizza parlors and in restaurants and by bombs aimed indiscriminately. But I never expected our president to give comfort to the enemy and inspire them.

I feel sorry for all the children of the world who will have to deal with the mess that we are now in. Anne and I send you wishes for the safety of you and Rosalynn and thank you for all your past efforts of helping the world.

Sincerely,
Kirk Douglas

If you look at a globe of the earth you will have a hard time finding Israel. It's a thin sliver of land hugging the Mediterranean Sea surrounded by Lebanon, Syria, Jordan, and Egypt. Beyond them lie Iraq, Iran, and Saudi Arabia — all enemies of Israel. Alone, Israel battled their combined forces in six wars, and with the help of God, they won each time. This could be Israel's battle cry:

O God, do not hold still;
Do not be deaf;
Do not be silent, O God!
For see — Your enemies rage,
And Your haters rear their heads.

Against Your people they conspire in secret;
They plot against those You shelter.
They say: "Come, and let us wipe out this nation,
So Israel's name is remembered no more."

President Carter was gracious enough to answer:

To Kirk Douglas,
I am sorry that you disagree with me about Israel's massive missile and bombing attack on Lebanon, with very high civilian casualties. Despite this, it should be obvious that the highest common commitment you and I have is for Israelis to be able to live in peace with all their neighbors. I have devoted a good portion of my life to this goal for more than thirty years. Israel has been relatively secure because of the never-violated peace treaty that was negotiated with Egypt in 1978 and 1979.

As you know, U.S. official policy, United Nations resolutions, the International Quartet's Road Map, and a majority of Israelis all agree that Israel must swap the occupied land for peace and that its neighbors and other Arabs must recognize Israel's right to live in peace within its legal borders. I hope that this will soon be possible.

Best wishes,
Jimmy

According to President Carter, Israel must give up land for peace. Remember when Neville Chamberlain went to Germany with his umbrella and visited Hitler at Berchtesgaden? In good faith, Chamberlain approved the surrender of the Sudetenland to the Nazis in order to attain peace. Hitler's next moves were to seize the rest of Czechoslovakia and invade Poland.

Israel gave up parts of the West Bank and dragged all the reluctant Jews out of Gaza. Did the sacrifice of land achieve peace? It is obvious that the enemies of Israel are not interested in the exchange of land for peace. Their goal is to nullify Israel's existence.

Hezbollah and Hamas echoed the call of Mahmoud Ahmadinejad, the leader of Iran: "Wipe Israel off the map." When Hezbollah shot rockets into Israel from Lebanon, Israel did what it has always done — fight back. If Israel were wiped off the map, the last outpost of democracy in that region of the world would be eliminated. Released from their gigantic burden of dealing with Israel, what would Hezbollah and Hamas do next?

President Carter is a religious man. He teaches Sunday school. He knows the Bible better than I do. He has visited Israel — the Holy Land — many times. He negotiated a peace treaty between Israel and Egypt.

I wonder what his reaction was the first time he saw the Dome of the Rock in Jerusalem glistening in the sun on the Temple Mount, the highest point in the city, which is under the control of Palestinians. At the base of the mount are the crumbling walls of the second temple — the Kotel, the Wailing Wall. Pious Jews come each day to pray, and visitors write their prayers on slips of paper and insert them in the crevices of the wall. Did President Carter offer a prayer? I have put four prayers in the wall over the years, and two of them were answered.

Did Carter visit Masada? Centuries ago, the Jews retreated to Masada, a high plateau not far from Jerusalem, when they were under attack by the Romans. For three years, they were surrounded by the Roman legion below. Finally, the Jews gave up and all of them committed suicide. When the Romans climbed up to Masada, they found no one alive. Today all Israeli officers, when they have completed their military training, climb up to Masada and swear an oath: "Never again! We will die fighting!"

President Carter suggests that we should follow the Camp David Accord — the 1978 peace treaty between Israel and Egypt, a major reason Carter received the Nobel Peace Prize in 2002. It was a success because the Egyptian leader, Anwar Sadat, surprised the world by taking a forty-five-minute flight to Jerusalem and convincing Prime Minister Menachem Begin to return the entire Sinai — an area larger than the whole state of Israel — to Egypt. Sadat's reward was to be assassinated by one of his own people.

I knew Sadat. When my wife and I were in Egypt, he invited us to visit him at Ismailia on the Suez Canal. What a charming man. If there were other leaders of his caliber in the Muslim Middle Eastern states, we would have peace. I also met with his wife, Jehan, and their family in Cairo. They had a beautiful daughter, whom I encouraged to become an actress, but she was too smart for that.

I saw Mrs. Sadat several times in the United States as well. Often, she was in the company of another widow, Leah Rabin, the wife of Prime Minister Yitzhak Rabin. Like Sadat, Rabin was also assassinated by one of his countrymen.

There has been an uproar over President Carter's book. One example is the full-page ad that was placed in the *New York Times* on December 28, 2006, by the nonpartisan group the Committee for Accuracy in Middle East Reporting in America. The headline was "Correct Carter's Falsehoods."

Kenneth W. Stein, now a professor at Emory University, was an adviser to Jimmy Carter and an executive director of the Carter Center for twenty-three years. He resigned his position, and fourteen other members of the Carter Center advisory board also resigned in protest of President Carter's new book. Professor Stein said in the *New York Times* on December 7, 2006, that Carter's book was "replete with factual errors, copied materials not cited, superficialities, glaring omissions, and simply invented segments."

President Carter placed the Medal of Freedom around my neck in 1981 in recognition of the work my wife and I had done for the United States Information Agency, speaking to university groups around the world about the United States. I was very proud that day and I had a warm feeling for the president and his wife. We became friends. He invited us to the White House, and we were honored to sleep in the Lincoln Bedroom and have breakfast with the president and Rosalynn in the morning. Years later, I attended his birthday party at the Carter Center in Atlanta. A few years ago, he surprised Anne and me with an afternoon visit at our home in Beverly Hills. It was such a friendly visit.

President Carter does a great job around the world, and I still continue to support his efforts, but I am shocked when I visit the Carter Center Web site. In the list of the center's major contributors are Prince Alaweed bin Talal, the Sultanate of Oman; Sultan Quobos bin Said al Said, the Kingdom of Saudi Arabia; Bakir M. bin Ladin of the Saudi bin Ladin Group; the Saudi Fund for Development; and the Government of the United Arab Emirates. How could I be a part of this group? Some of these people and their associates are among those who are fomenting vicious anti-Israeli hatred around the world.

I pick up Carter's book, *Palestine: Peace Not Apartheid.* On the cover, a large photo of the former president looks thoughtfully at a spliced-in photograph of part of the barrier wall that separates Israelis from

Palestinians in the West Bank. He is deep in thought and seems to be looking over the wall toward the Israeli side. At the base of the wall, hordes of Palestinians are marching in a demonstration against their neighbor.

It makes me very sad. Let's face it, I lost a friend, but Israel has gained an enemy.

48
SUNSET

A few leaves from the avocado tree are falling to the ground. I am in my garden on a December evening, not quite alone. I have a half-empty glass of vodka. It's cool and I'm wearing a sweater. I feel irritable; I don't know why. I get up and carefully carry my drink around the pool to the dual bust. I look at the heads once again. The young Kirk seems to be hiding in the evening shadows so I stare at the arrogant face of the older Kirk.

"Are you a Jew? You don't look Jewish."

How often have people said that to me? Was it an insult or a compliment? I sip my drink.

I continue talking. "Hey, Jew boy! I'm talking to you, Issur Danielovitch! Yeah! That's your real name! Who changed it to Izzy Demsky? Some improvement!"

He stares back at me defiantly, his chin jutting out. In the dim light, his dimple looks like a deep cave.

"*You* changed it to Kirk Douglas. Remember? Became a movie star — made a lot of money. Do you hear me? I'm talking to you! *Answer* me!"

I slap his face. It makes a hollow sound and stings my hand.

"Honey, are you talking to yourself?" Anne calls from the house.

"Yes, I am!"

"Well, when you finish, dinner is ready."

I feel silly. As I raise my glass, it slips out of my hands and shatters on the deck. I look down at the shards of glass and mutter to myself, "The world is broken."

I hobble toward the house, still muttering.

At the top of the steps I stop, turn around, and look at old Kirk. The evening dew seems to form tears on his cheeks. I'm sorry I slapped him. I tell him: "Please don't cry. But we must do something to help other people. If you save one person, you've saved the world, a world madly out of control. It's time for *tikkun olam* — repair the world. No matter how old you are, we must try."

I hear a scratching on the glass door. Danny and Foxy are impatient for me to enter. I saw them only five minutes ago. Now they greet me as if I'd been gone for a year. I slide open the door, and they jump all over me, tails wagging furiously. They follow me into my den.

"Kirk!"

"I'll be ready in five minutes, Anne." I go to the bathroom and splash cold water on my face. I lean my head against the mirror, as the dogs watch me patiently. The cool glass feels good against my skin. I straighten up and look at myself — old Kirk, with white hair and wrinkled face. I mutter,

Grow old along with me!
The best is yet to be . . .

Well, I'm waiting. I'm still waiting.

EPILOGUE

At home after my nintieth birthday party, I washed my face thoroughly, looked in the mirror, and studied my wrinkles and silver-gray head. I thought of the streaks of gray I had seen in my sons' hair at the party. A time will come when they will all match my head of gray. I will never see it. I climbed into bed, the one secure place in the world, and pulled the covers over me. I felt safe and waited for my wife. Why do women need more time to get undressed for bed than they need to get dressed to go out?

Anne entered the room. "Ninety, ugh . . . to think I'm married to such an old man."

"Honey," I said, "the party was beautiful."

"Oh, thank you. I know how much you hate birthday parties, but I think this one really worked, don't you? Everyone had a great time."

"Everyone had a great time because I was the oldest man there."

Anne laughed. "But you seemed so young when you recited that poem — without notes!"

"I learned it in college."

Anne sat on the bed and leaned over. "How many girls did you recite that poem to?"

"Honey, how could I ever say those lines to another girl and mean it?"

"Because you're a pretty good actor."

I clasped her hand and said:

For thy sweet love remember'd such
    wealth brings
That then I scorn to change my state with
    kings.

Her eyes were moist as she put her arms around me. Her good night kiss was sweet, long, and tender. It made me tingle. She hugged me tightly and whispered in my ear, "I love you, Kirk — I love you very much."

She lifted her head and looked at me. I saw that her eyes were welling up with tears. She whispered, "Good night, darling," and quickly got up, turned off the lights, and closed the door. She has never liked me to see her cry.

I rolled over, still tingling.

Let's face it — ninety isn't so bad.

CREDITS

Text

Page 95: Al Pacino's letter to Kirk Douglas dated December 6, 2006, is used by kind permission of Al Pacino.

Page 136: "A Whale of a Tale" from Walt Disney's 20,000 LEAGUES UNDER THE SEA, Words and Music by Norman Gimbel and Al Hoffman. Copyright © 1953 by Wonderland Music Company, Inc. Copyright renewed. All rights reserved. Used by permission.

Pages 154–155: "A Bushel and a Peck" from GUYS AND DOLLS by Frank Loesser. Copyright © 1950 (Renewed) by FRANK MUSIC CORP. All rights reserved.

Pages 196–197: "Let Me Live Out My Years" by John G. Neihardt from "A Bundle of Myrrh" in *Lyric and Dramatic Poems.* Copyright © 1907. Used by permission of the John G. Neihardt Trust.

Pages 242–243: "Does It Matter?" by Sieg-

Insert Photos

Page 1: Private collection.

Page 2 (top): Private collection.

Page 2 (bottom): Private collection, photograph by William Reed Woodfield.

Page 3: Private collection.

Page 4 (top): Copyright © 1952 by Warner Bros. Entertainment Inc. All rights reserved. Used by permission.

Page 4 (bottom): Copyright © 1956 by Warner Bros. Entertainment Inc. All rights reserved. Used by permission.

Page 5 (top): Private collection.

Page 5 (bottom): Official White House photo.

Page 6 (both): Official White House photo.

Page 7 (both): Private collection.

Page 8: Copyright © 2006 by Annie Leibovitz/Contact Press Images.

Page 9 (top): Private collection, photograph by Peggy Peattie.

Page 9 (bottom): Private collection.

Page 10 (top): Private collection.

Page 10 (bottom) Private collection, photograph by Barbara Alessandra.

Page 11 (top): Copyright © by Mark Abraham.

Page 11 (bottom): Private collection.

Page 12: Private collection, photograph by Michael Jacobs.

Page 13 (top): Photo courtesy of Jolene Schlatter.

Page 13 (bottom): Private collection.

Page 14: Copyright © by Reto Guntli/Burda Verlag/Home&Style.

Page 15: Private collection.

Page 16 (top): Private collection.

Page 16 (bottom): Photo courtesy of Mike Abrums.

Page 17 (both): Private collection, photograph by Michael Jacobs.

Page 18: Private collection, photograph by Michael Jacobs.

Page 19 (top): Private collection.

Page 19 (bottom): Copyright © 2006 by Jesse and William Johnson. Used by permission.

Page 20 (both): Private collection, photograph by Alex Berliner.

Page 21: Private collection, photograph by Janos Kovesdi.

Page 22 (top): Private collection, photograph by Barbara Alessandra.

Page 22 (bottom): Private collection.

Page 23: Private collection, photograph by Christopher Briscoe.

Page 24: Private collection.

ABOUT THE AUTHOR

Kirk Douglas has been a household name for six decades. He has appeared in more than eighty films and has been nominated for an Academy Award for *Champion, The Bad and the Beautiful,* and *Lust for Life.* Douglas received the Presidential Medal of Freedom in 1981, a special Oscar in 1996, and the National Medal of the Arts in 2001. He is the author of three previous bestselling memoirs, three novels, and two children's books.

The employees of Thorndike Press hope you have enjoyed this Large Print book. All our Thorndike and Wheeler Large Print titles are designed for easy reading, and all our books are made to last. Other Thorndike Press Large Print books are available at your library, through selected bookstores, or directly from us.

For information about titles, please call:
  (800) 223-1244

or visit our Web site at:
  www.gale.com/thorndike
  www.gale.com/wheeler

To share your comments, please write:
  Publisher
  Thorndike Press
  295 Kennedy Memorial Drive
  Waterville, ME 04901